# Stepparent to Stepparent

# Stepparent to Stepparent

## Answers to 50 Common Questions Stepparents Ask

**Margaret Broersma**

*Stepparent to Stepparent: Answers to 50 Common Questions Stepparents Ask*



Published by Kregel Publications, a division of Kregel, Inc., P.O. Box 2607, Grand Rapids, MI 49501.



Cover design: John M. Lucas

ISBN 0-8254-2208-6

Printed in the United States of America

04 05 06 07 08 / 5 4 3 2 1

*To my husband*
*Thank you for being my partner—*
*in not giving up and in reaping*
*the harvest.*

Let us not become weary in doing good, for at the proper time we will reap a harvest if we do not give up.
—*Galatians 6:9*

Perseverance must finish its work so that you may be mature and complete, not lacking anything.
—*James 1:4*

# Contents

# Preface

I'm a stepparent with more than seventeen years of experience in blending a family and we have seen God's faithfulness every step of the way. In *Stepparent to Stepparent* I share with you from my experience, as well as from the experiences of many couples with whom my husband Roger and I have worked in our support groups and workshops.

Many people have written to us asking for advice. Their letters comprise the foundation of this book and have been edited for brevity, anonymity, and inclusiveness. Some letters in this book are not derived from actual correspondence, but rather from the most common discussion questions in the support groups we have led.

My prayer is that this book will be a support and guide for your stepfamily.

*This book makes no statement about divorce. Rather, it speaks to reality—nearly half of the families in the United States, including those within the church, are blended and struggle in ways that need to be addressed.*

*Please note that the advice in this book is not a substitute for professional counseling.*

Chapter 1

# Blended Names

## *Question*

Dear Margaret,

My precious young son has begun to call his stepfather "Dad." This breaks my heart because becoming a dad was the most important experience of my life. The thought of my child calling someone else by my name seems unbearable. I am a father who is very involved with my child, and the divorce was not my idea. My ex-wife says I am being overly sensitive and that our child can call her husband anything he wants, although I'm sure she encourages him to do it. I say "Dad" is a special name for a special relationship, and I would like it to be reserved for me.

Am I being overly sensitive? What can I do?

Signed,
A Good Dad, USA

## *Response*

Dear Good Dad,

I agree that being a dad is a very special thing. Your letter reflects your hurt and my heart goes out to you. Most of the birthdads we know reserve the name "Dad" for themselves, and most stepkids we know, whose birthparents are *involved in their lives,* call their stepparents by their first names.

*But*—you cannot control your ex-wife and what she may or may not encourage your son to do. I suggest that you sit down with your child and as simply as possible, explain to him that it hurts your feelings to hear him call his stepfather "Dad." Also, if it's possible to do so in a calm and nonthreatening way, you may have one more talk with your ex, explaining your feelings to her as well.

*Then don't bring it up again.* You don't want your child to have to choose sides. If he knows you want one thing and his mother wants another, he'll feel conflicted and guilty. If these feelings always accompany a visit with you, he may want to avoid the pain by avoiding a visit.

You have a special bond with your son and no one can take that away, no matter what name he calls his stepdad. Keep on being an involved, loving dad and you'll never lose your child's loyalty and love.

Remember to let God, the perfect parent, parent you when you need it! You can get further encouragement by reading devotion number 89 from my book *Daily Reflections for Stepparents.*[1]

*The LORD your God is with you,*
*he is mighty to save.*
*He will take great delight in you,*
*he will quiet you with his love,*
*he will rejoice over you with singing.*
—*Zephaniah 3:17*

All the best,
Margaret

## *Question*

Dear Margaret,

As an engaged couple, we are looking forward to our wedding and to blending our families. We have four children between us, and have custody of them all. They are ages four, five, six, and eight. We hope to have a child together. Each of our kids sees their birthparents only every other weekend and sometimes extra for holidays. Since we'll all be living together most of the time, we think all the kids should call us "Mom" and "Dad," regardless of whether or not they are our birthkids. But the kids' birthparents got angry when we suggested this. And, in all honesty, we don't want to confuse the children either. So far, the future stepkids have been calling us by our first names. But we want to be a real family, so what should we have the children call us?

Eager to Be Mom and Dad

## *Response*

Dear Mom and Dad,

I'm happy for you—congratulations! As you can see from the letter above, your desire to be called "Mom" and "Dad" by your stepchildren may be painful for your ex-spouses. Most of the stepkids whom I know call their stepparents by their first names. But in some cases, when the children are young, as yours are, I've heard of some wonderfully creative approaches to the name dilemma. *Be assured, no matter what name you are called by your stepchildren, you will be a family—a unique blended family designed by all of you.*

One stepmom we know is called "Mom" by her stepkids, while they reserve "Mama" or "Mommy" for their birthmother. Another family that we know of has been together for twenty years and is very well blended and completely bonded. When the couple first got married they called a family meeting about the issue of what names to use for their

**Although names may be an emotional issue when the family is first blending, the name by which the children call you has little to do with how your relationship will turn out.**

stepparents. The kids picked the name "Pa" for their stepdad, reserving "Dad" for their birthfather. In this particular family, the grown daughter says that her pa is her real parent. It seems her dad checked out of her life when he left her mom, and she feels that "Pa" has done a great job of raising her. On the other hand, we know a stepdad who's always been called "Dad" by his stepkids, as they had no other father, yet they have a chaotic and insecure relationship. We know of a favorite stepgrandma who's "Mee-ma" and a beloved grandpa who is "Pee-pa."

The point is, although names may be an emotional issue when the family is first blending, the name by which the children call you has little to do with how your relationship will turn out. Your children are old enough to sit down with you and talk about this. We're glad you've already done some talking, but if you can't come up with something special with which you'll all feel comfortable, don't worry about it. Your first names will do just fine, as long as you both expect and receive the respect you need to be the parents in your blended home.

A word of caution: you *are* a blended family. Because your children are young and live primarily with you, you may be tempted to dream that you'll eventually become "the same" as a nuclear family. You won't. To hope so is setting yourself up for disappointment. A birthparent who deserves respect and consideration will probably always be in the picture. You can show love to your kids and stepkids most effectively by encouraging these relationships to be as healthy and consistent as possible. Strive for open, cooperative, and peaceable relationships with your ex-spouses. This will most benefit the children.

Even when a birthparent is deceased, we encourage stepparents to treat the memory of that parent with respect, and to allow the children to go on loving that parent without guilt.

No matter what your stepchildren call you, "may the Lord make your love increase and overflow for each other" (1 Thess. 3:12).

God bless you!
Margaret

Chapter 2

# Winning Your Stepchild

## *Question*

Dear Margaret,

I'm a stepdad, and no matter what I do, my teenage stepdaughter hates me. She says it's her goal to get me out of the house! I don't know why she should hate me so much. I treat both her and her mother well. How can I get her to like me? I feel like I must win her over soon, or I'll begin to hate her back. The way she treats me really hurts.

Just sign me,
Rejected Stepdad

Please read on.

## *Question*

Dear Margaret,

I'm a stepmom, and before the wedding I thought I really loved my stepkids. Now, as we live together, they reject my hugs, ignore my discipline, and sometimes even ignore me. I feel myself resenting, maybe even hating them. I feel guilty for saying this, but when they sass and do nothing to cooperate, hateful emotions bubble up in me. If I have to hear, "I don't have to—you're not my mom" one more time, I think I'll be utterly destroyed! Help!

I'm a,
Rejected Stepmom

## *Response*

Dear Rejected Stepparents,

For the kids, the honeymoon is over the minute the birthparent and the stepparent begin living together. Yes, rejection hurts, especially when it's from someone who's such an important part of our lives. But you are not alone. Almost every stepparent we know has experienced rejection to some degree. My husband Roger and I are no exception.

**You're not the birthparent, but you *are* the mom or the dad of this house.**

First, establish who you are. The bottom line is, you are not your stepkids' birthparent, and you never will be. Another dad/mom will always be in your stepkids' lives. Even a deceased parent is often referred to as "my real mom" or "my real dad." And that's okay! You are not inferior nor are you worthless in your stepkids' lives. Right now, your role and meaning in their lives is just beginning. No, you're not the birthparent, but you *are* the mom or the dad of this house. Say it. Have your spouse say it. Then act like it. No, you're not your stepkids' birthparent, but you're the mom and the dad who are there, now, in that place—and you'll be respected as such when you and your spouse demand this respect.

Most of us, though, want more than respect. We want a close bond with our stepchildren. But often—just when we're beginning to feel the closest to our stepchildren—they'll do something that seems meant to sabotage the relationship. Our family counselor advised that when the kids began to really love us they felt guilty, because loving us made them feel disloyal to their birthparents. The kids need to actually hear, "I'm the mom/dad who is here, in this house, but I'm not replacing your birthparent. I'm the mom/dad who is here, but I know you'll always love your other parent." Simply don't compete. Assure your stepkids that they may love both their birthparent and you, too. Teach them that *love is not finite.*

**What does it mean to choose love? *Real love in action is commitment.***

Second, establish your role for the individual child. If the children are young, you may have to act as an actual parent to them, caring for their physical needs and doing the hands-on chores of raising them. In this case, you need to also be a disciplinarian—a complete parent. (See the next chapter.) If, however, the children are older, you—as a stepparent—may be more of a friend or a mentor. No matter what your role, you should expect and receive respect, and your spouse should be prepared to dish out previously agreed upon consequences if you do not get this respect.

Third, don't worry about your feelings. It's normal to have negative feelings when you are being treated poorly, but you don't have to act upon those feelings. *As the adult, you can choose to be loving, fair, and kind, regardless of how you feel.*

Finally, of utmost importance, know that *there's no such thing as instant love.* Just because you married your stepchildren's mom or dad, doesn't mean you automatically love your stepchildren. *But,* as stated, you can choose to act in a loving way—and over time love will grow.

**Just like any friendship, your relationship with your stepchild will grow only if you spend time together.**

What does it mean to choose love? *Real love in action is commitment* and the daily choices we make to honor that commitment. We love what our friend told his teenage stepdaughter when she screamed at him, "My goal is to get you out of this house!" He answered calmly, "It's good to have a goal." In the face of her adolescent anger and emotion, he responded with love or, when appropriate, ignored her outbursts. As his stepdaughter saw his continued commitment to both her and her mom, when she learned that day after day he came home to them, she began to trust him. Now, five years later, she loves her stepdad and has asked him to give her away at her wedding.

Over time, as you give and demand mutual respect, as you create a shared life, as you make memories (see the chapter on "Blending Traditions"), as time passes and you find a way to live together, feelings of love and affection will grow. It takes time and an act of the will to do things that will build your relationship.

Yes, it takes time for love to grow, but you need to *make* time to make it happen. Just like any friendship, your relationship with your stepchild will grow only if you spend time together. You can work together, play together, and build memories together.

One of the best ways to grow family relationships is through the sharing of ourselves. Here are some ideas:

*Write notes of love and kindness.* A stepmom I know got a warm response from a difficult stepdaughter when she put fresh flowers in the teenager's room with a note that said, "I prayed for you today." Sometimes, when my own blended family had a rough morning getting ready, I'd go to school and put notes of encouragement in the kids' lockers.

*When you have to go on an errand or do an outdoor task, take a kid along.* When the kids were little in our family, a favorite thing on Saturdays was being chosen to go to the hardware store with Roger or be taken out to coffee with him and his brothers.

*Take advantage of the moment.* As you share of yourself, encourage the children to share in return. It doesn't take a lot of planning and scheming to build a relationship. Ask the kids about their day. Be there for their special events like sports, concerts, and plays. Praise their accomplishments, hug them, hold them, pray with them and for them.

*Be sensitive to their comfort levels.* A friend of mine hugged her older stepchildren at night before bed just as she hugged her own. One night she realized her stepson was avoiding her, purposefully keeping away from her hug. So she learned to give what she calls "hidden hugs." Whenever she could, she gave him positive verbal feedback. When joking around, she ruffled his hair or, when he needed encouragement, gave him a pat on the back. As time passed, he began to be more open and today, six years later, my friend and her stepson have built a warm relationship.

**As stepparents, we find it most crucial to love with God's love.**

*Worship together.* A time of real blending for our family occurred as we sat around the dinner table, having devotions together. We'd read an age-appropriate Bible story or Scripture, and talk about how it applied to life. To illustrate the Bible truth, we often shared stories of our past lives, including memories of our kids' other parent. We talked about how God has been and is being faithful to us.

As all of this sharing of ourselves takes place, feelings of love and affection will grow.

To sum up: don't expect instant love. Choose love, even when you don't feel it. Take time to let time bond you. And one more thing: without the love of God within us, His Spirit loving through us, we can't imagine learning to love our stepchildren. As stepparents, we find it most crucial to love with God's love.

> *I have loved you with an everlasting love;*
> *I have drawn you with loving-kindness.*
>
> —*Jeremiah 31:3*

> *This is how God showed his love among us: He sent his one and only Son into the world that we might live through him. This is love: not that we loved God, but that he loved us and sent his Son as an atoning sacrifice for our sins. Dear friends, since God so loved us, we also ought to love one another. No one has ever seen God; but if we love one another, God lives in us and his love is made complete in us. We know that we live in him and he in us, because he has given us of his Spirit.*
>
> *—1 John 4:9–13*

May you grow in love for your children and stepchildren as you grow in love for the Lord,
Margaret

Chapter 3

# Blending Discipline

## *Question*

Dear Margaret,

I'm a stepmother to two teenage stepdaughters, and they're truly "stepdaughters from hell." For the most part they totally ignore me, won't even look at me, and usually don't answer when I speak to them. If I ask them to pick up after themselves, do a chore, or even do something as simple as take off their shoes because I just cleaned the floor, they scream obscenities at me. They've even tried to hit me when I ask them to pick up.

The last straw came a week ago when they spit in my glass of lemonade. When I went berserk about it, they each had their boyfriend sneak into my bathroom and urinate into my shampoo. One of them actually placed other bodily fluids in my conditioner. When I asked my husband to intervene, he said that I was overreacting and that I need to be more forgiving. Needless to say, after this I took my own two kids and moved out.

My husband is a kind and loving man, and we can't really afford living separately. I really want to be with him, but not with his kids. What can I do?

I'm,
Desperate in Detroit

## *Response*

Dear Desperate,

You've been living under a tremendous amount of pressure. You're right—your stepdaughters' behavior has been extreme, and the things they have done are horrid. I can see why you needed to take a break. You had to protect yourself, your sanity, and your own children. Cooling down periods can be good, but remember, this man comes with kids—they're not going to disappear. Most experts agree, the most difficult relationship in a blended family is that of stepmom and stepdaughter. This is especially true if the daughters are teens.

**Most experts agree, the most difficult relationship in a blended family is that of stepmom and stepdaughter.**

Children of divorce are grieving losses, and they often show the grief and loss through anger. Their family of origin has broken apart, and with you on the scene there's no hope of their birthparents ever getting back together. It probably wasn't their idea for their dad to remarry. Maybe they liked things just the way they were—with their dad all to themselves. Do you see why they resent you?

Initially, the only person who can talk to these girls on your behalf is your husband. Perhaps you need to ask yourself if he's really the kind and wonderful man you believe him to be when he allows his children to treat his wife with such disrespect. He's the one who must set limits with them and make perfectly clear what behavior is acceptable and what is not acceptable in his home. And the unacceptable behavior must have consequences. He may benefit from counseling on how to set boundaries with his kids.

You cannot control what your husband does, though, nor can you control (as you have well seen) what your stepdaughters do. You can, however, control your reaction to their behavior. A counselor should be able to help you change the way you respond to your stepdaughters, which may in turn change their behavior.

Remember, though, that the kids are teens. In just a few short years they'll be gone. If you're sure this is the man with whom you want to spend your retirement years, you can choose to stay with him. But everyone will need to make some changes to make your home life more workable now. Is your husband willing to make some changes? Are you?

**I don't know how anyone could survive stepparenting without the Word of God for wisdom and encouragement.**

Another thing to ask yourself is this: "How is this atmosphere affecting my own children? Do I want them to grow up in this house with these people?" All of this hostility can't be good for them. Again, a counselor can help you understand how this environment is affecting your kids and how you can do what's best for them.

If you decide to stay in this marriage, all of you will need family counseling to make it work. Look in the yellow pages under family counselors and speak with them on the phone to see if they counsel all family members on blending issues. Some health insurance plans pay for this, and many counseling services charge on an income-based, sliding scale. You and your husband could also benefit from a stepparent support group. Look for one in your area by calling family services or by contacting the Stepfamily Association of America online (see Resources list in back of this book). They have chapters in most states. They also have listings of approved counselors.

One more thing—I don't know how anyone could survive stepparenting without the Word of God for wisdom and encouragement.

To help you focus on the words of God, use our books *Devotions for the Blended Family* and *Daily Reflections for Stepparents.*[1] Meditating on a proverb a day also can help you cope. That's what I did when I became a stepmother to three stepdaughters. Doing so changed my way of thinking, which also changed my feelings.

Please read the letters that follow for more coping ideas.

> *But if from there you seek the* Lord *your God, you will find him if you look for him with all your heart and with all your soul. When you are in distress and all these things have happened to you, then in later days you will return to the* Lord *your God and obey him. For the* Lord *your God is a merciful God; he will not abandon or destroy you or forget the covenant.*
>
> —*Deuteronomy 4:29–31*

May God bless you and heal you,
Margaret

## *Question*

Dear Margaret,

I need help! My husband and I are newly married. We've known each other for several years, and I've known his children just as long. We thought our kids were great friends—and then we got married. The problem is, his children have no discipline. He lets them do whatever they want, and they have no respect for anyone.

When his children were here before the wedding, his daughter ripped up my daughter's doll. Then when my daughter wore one of his daughter's old, outgrown tops, she beat my daughter with a rod. His son kept picking on (jumping on) my daughter. She warned him several times to stop, and he didn't. Finally, she beat the daylights out of him.

My husband doesn't say anything to his kids about this stuff unless it's to talk baby talk to them. His daughter is nine and his son is thirteen, but he acts as if they're little babies who don't know any better.

We were going to take a family vacation, but now my husband's son is coming for two weeks and my kids are refusing to go on a vacation with this awful boy. Can you blame them? Who knows what he'll do?

I'm rapidly beginning to hate these two kids, who I used to really like. Can you help?

Just sign me,
Broken Dreams

## *Response*

Dear Broken,

Try to think for a moment from the kids' point of view. Their dad, who they come to visit—*their* dad, who they see only a few times a year—is living with some other kids . . . kids who get to see him every day! He's married to you, which means there's no longer a chance that he'll get back with their mom (a fantasy most kids of a broken marriage feel at some point). So they're grieving and angry because their family will never be a family again, and their dad sort of belongs to these other kids now. They resent you because you're the one who "changed everything." Can you imagine the rejection, hurt, and anger they must feel? Anytime they can get him to take their side in a disagreement is one moment they know he's still their dad—loyal to them.

**Clearly established boundaries with clearly set consequences actually make the kids feel secure and loved.**

Perhaps he treats them as babies because he's reverting to a time when he *knew* how to relate to them. So much has changed and, like most people in a newly blended family, he simply doesn't know what to do. Like almost every father of divorce we've met, your husband sees his children so seldom he hates to be "the heavy." He is afraid to discipline because then maybe they won't like him, and it would kill him if his kids rejected him.

The good news is, clearly established boundaries with clearly set consequences actually make the kids feel secure and loved. You can tell them this! They're old enough to understand that the boundaries you set and the consequences for disobedience you create are for their own good. They will actually feel more a part of the family if everyone, including them, has to live by the same rules.

The behavior of those children is, indeed, troublesome, making it easy to think that they don't deserve to be loved or treated well. But none of us, in fact, deserves God's love. The Bible says, "We love him, because he first loved us" (1 John 4:19 KJV); and "Love one another; as I have loved you" (John 13:34 KJV). How did God love me? He loved me so much, He sent His son to die for me before I even gave Him the time of day. He loved me while I was still bad, still in my sins. He loved me *before I loved Him* (see Rom. 5:8)!

**For the security of the children, and for the sanity of everyone, the entire family needs to know the limits of behavior in your house.**

*Pray for God to fill you with love and compassion for your stepkids, even though they don't deserve it.* No, you won't feel for them like you do for your own. But you are the adult, and you can, with the help of God, *choose* to be loving, kind, fair, and firm, even when they don't deserve it and you don't feel like it.

While we encourage love and compassion, *we also encourage sane limit-setting with* all *the kids in the family, and sensible consequences* for violations of those limits. For the security of the children, and for the sanity of everyone, the entire family needs to know the limits of behavior in your house. Together, *behind closed doors,* you and your husband *need to come to an understanding* about a family plan. Then take the plan to the kids. Listen to their input. Be willing to make adjustments in areas that can be flexible. Some areas, of course, are not debatable.

For example, "All acts of physical abuse are off limits. If one of you kids hurts another, the consequence will be ___________." You fill in the blank. *The rules are the same for all.* There are no second chances when a stated rule has been violated, and *all receive the same consequence.* Some blended families benefit from an objective third party, like a counselor, who helps them to make a family plan such as this.

**One of the biggest needs of birthchildren is more time alone with their birthparents.**

If you really believe that the stress of a vacation together would be too much to handle, then you may make the decision to put it off—or you may decide, just this once, to have separate vacations—he with his kids and you with yours. Our social worker told us that one of the biggest needs of birthchildren is more time alone with their birthparents.

If you decide to go together, you need to establish ground rules. You would say to your children, "Now, about this trip—there's no question and no argument—all of us are going. It's a family vacation." Be clear that neither his children nor yours are the bosses in your home. You are the mom and your husband is the dad *in this house.*

But you also want to give all the children some choices and some guarantee of safety, so at vacation time you'll need to review the rules for behavior and remind all the kids of the consequences. Be clear about what will happen if you don't get what you expect on this trip. Give them some choices about the actual things you'll do while on vacation. Perhaps each person can choose an activity. When we went to a famous amusement park, for example, we allowed each kid to pick his or her favorite ride, and we all rode it again together.

Assure all the children that you love them and that you will do your best to be fair to everyone. Do everything you can to make each person feel that he or she has a part in the planning and the doing of this vacation. Try to make it something that draws the family together rather than pushes you apart. And, again, you may decide that things are too stressful now and this trip will have to wait for next year.

Get some loving and open communication going on a daily basis. Give hugs and compliments as often as possible to birthkids as well as stepkids. Give equal responsibilities to everyone and praise each child when he or she carries them out. In other words, take *active steps* to make your household become a blended family.

To help you in your family discussions, you may want to use our book *Devotions for the Blended Family.*[2] It includes common questions that come up in relation to the kids, what God's Word has to say on the subject, and discussion questions that can help get you all talking.

Remember, "If any of you lacks wisdom, he [she] should ask God, who gives generously to all without finding fault, and it will be given to him [her]" (James 1:5).

May God give you wisdom!
Margaret

## *Question*

Dear Margaret,

I have a problem with my thirteen-year-old son and my husband of three years. My son will not respect my husband or myself anymore (he used to), and he has a lot of anger toward us, which shows all the time. We've had problems in our relationship in the past and have twice almost ended it with divorce. At these times, my children and I moved into a rental house. Each time, I returned to my husband, which I'm sure left the kids plenty confused.

Now my son has decided to move in with his father because he can no longer stand his stepfather. I'm trying to stop this move because rules are looser there—no limits on TV shows, no controls on computer sites, no enforced bed time.

Whenever my son comes home from a visit, he's mean and rude

to both of us, which in turn leads to our fighting for days because my husband accuses me of raising him so badly. I must admit, his grades have gone down so far that I'm afraid he is going to fail, and his friends are now a group of really "bad boyz." So we're in constant turmoil when he's here, and I'm terrified of letting him go. What should I do?

I am,
A Very Scared and Torn Mom

## *Response*

Dear Mom,

I'm glad to hear that you and your husband are working out the problems in your marriage. We hope that you've gotten help to do this. The most common reason for second divorces is conflict over the children, but one day the kids will all be gone, and your marriage relationship is what will be left. Nurture it! A strong marriage also makes for a secure home for all who live there.

**One day the kids will all be gone, and your marriage relationship is what will be left.**

It's quite common for the birthparent to feel torn between his or her child and a new spouse. Also, adolescent boys reach a stage when they need to live with their fathers. It feels like a great loss to you, because you've raised this boy yourself. But as he becomes a man, it's normal and healthy for him to separate from his mother and identify with his father. Doing so is a necessary step toward heterosexual manhood. Male children—even those in their original, in-tact families—eventually hang out more with the guys and spend less time with their mothers.

You need to let him go. You're right—the off and on conflict with your husband has made him angry, which is making his rebellion worse. He probably took your side when you had conflicts with your husband, probably even feeling like your protector. When you went back to your husband, he felt angry toward his stepdad, and possibly as if he was on an emotional roller coaster. He needs stability, and you and your husband's marriage needs a break from his bad attitude and disobedience. Consider, too, your other children. They need some peace in their home. All the conflict with your son cannot be having a good effect upon them. They need a stable and secure home, and if your son's leaving will help, that's another reason to let him go.

***Stepparents can bring a wonderful objectivity, unhindered by protective emotion, to the problems of parenting.***

At the same time you let him go, give him completely over to God. Be gracious and loving, telling him that you love him so much it kills you to let him go, but you know it's something he needs to do, and you're going to let him do it. Don't be surprised, though, if he wants to come back.

How do you handle the differences in values and standards between your home and your ex-husband's home? Please read the next letter for my thoughts on this.

I hope that you and your husband are getting counseling, and with the help of an objective third party, you will now set reasonable and consistent guidelines for the rest of your children. Remember, reasonable and firm boundaries and expectations, combined with some areas of choice, make children feel secure.

For the sake of your marriage and family, it's important, too, that you respect the input of your husband when setting up the rules, boundaries, and responsibilities for the rest of the children in your home. *Stepparents can bring a wonderful objectivity, unhindered by protective emotion, to the problems of parenting.*

Listen to one another, and if you really want a blended home, let your husband share in the parenting of your children. Do your talking in private, and then present a united front to the children.

One final thing: *Never let your children act disrespectfully to your husband. Make sure that you give consequences when they do. It could save your marriage.*

Jesus said, "Peace I leave with you; my peace I give you. I do not give to you as the world gives. Do not let your hearts be troubled and do not be afraid" (John 14:27). And finally, "Cast all your anxiety on him because he cares for you" (1 Peter 5:7).

May Jesus bring you peace as you cast yourselves upon Him,
Margaret

## *Question*

Dear Margaret,

The divorce is long over; we have both remarried. My wife's eight-year-old daughter lives with us (she sees her dad every other weekend); I have shared custody of my two kids (a six-year-old daughter and an eight-year-old son); and we have one together, who is still a baby. The problem is, our children have totally different rules at our house than they have at their other birthparents' houses.

We go to church every weekend. When the kids are with their other parents, they don't. We expect them to help set the table, clean up after dinner, make their own beds, pick up their toys, and so forth. We limit what they watch on TV, and computer use is monitored for appropriateness. At their other birthparents' houses, both my wife's daughter and my son and daughter can watch whatever they want on TV, and no one pays any attention to them when they're on the computer (so they tell us when we remind them of our rules).

They're young now, but what will happen in the future? We're really worried.

Sign us,
Fearful of All Our Hard Work Being Undone

## *Response*

Dear Fearfuls,

The rules in one home being different from the rules in the other home is one of the most common problems in blended families. It sounds as if you and your wife have good communication, and that you've given a lot of thought to the kind of family and home that you want to have. Excellent.

**_Do not_ make your home stricter to try to make up for the other parents' leniency.**

Unfortunately, you can't control other people—you can't tell the other parents what to do, and really, as difficult as it may be to accept, each biological parent has the right to raise the children as he or she sees fit. We hope you'll have at least one chance to talk to your ex-spouses about these issues. Don't expect to change their standards, but do present yours and show them reasons why you do what you do. Ask them if they think some uniformity of rules and standards between homes is possible. You may be surprised that they actually agree on some things! Even in original, intact homes children try to play one parent off another to get their own way. The chances of them doing this are even greater in a blended family. So don't be surprised if this is what has been happening.

A couple from our support group became frustrated with one of the children saying things like, "My dad said at your house I don't have to do that"; or "My mom says I can do this if I like; I don't have to listen to you." They decided to sit him down with all four parents and talk. They were all amazed to hear that a nine-year-old could create such stories! Most of what he claimed was, of course, an attempt to get his own way. Each birthparent had to remind their son of the necessity of following the rules of the home he was in.

If this is not the case, and your children's other parents really do want the kids to live without rules and standards while with them, all you can do is be consistent and as fair as possible when they're in your home. *Do not* make your home stricter to try to make up for the other parents' leniency. But do obey Scripture and train up your children in the way that God would have them go. Pray and read the Bible or age-appropriate Christian material with your children every night that they're with you. As you have this devotional time together with God, their morality and character will be formed. For children the age that you mention, many wonderful Bible story books are on the market as well as books on developing Christian character. One book we recommend is *Leading Little Ones to God* by Marion Schooland.[3]

Each time the kids are scheduled for a visit with their other parents, pray with them before they go. Pray that they'll remember God's laws, and while they're gone, pray all the time for their spiritual protection. Trust your children to God.

Never be critical of the other parents in front of your children. *They need all of their parents, and they need to respect all of their parents.* It may help all of you to think about this: children have to deal with different rules wherever they go. The behavior guidelines for school, organized sports, and summer camp may all be different, but children everywhere are capable of adapting and following the rules when those rules are clearly presented. In the same way, children can learn that in their two homes things may be done differently, but they still must abide by the rules of each house. If you see them struggling with the inconsistencies, remind them that all of their parents want the best for them, but that "*in this house, this is the way we do it.*"

They may be grumpy or even angry when they first come home from a visit with their other parents. They're dealing with the loss of a parent every time they go from one place to the other. But as they grow up living in two places, they'll adapt to the differences in house rules and expectations. They'll see, if they don't already, that they have four parents who love them and care about them.

> *Hear, O Israel: The LORD our God, the LORD is one. Love the LORD your God with all your heart and with all your*

> *soul and with all your strength. These commandments that I give you today are to be upon your hearts. Impress them on your children. Talk about them when you sit at home and when you walk along the road, when you lie down and when you get up.*
>
> —*Deuteronomy 6:4–7*

May God bless your blended Christian home,
Margaret

## *Question*

Dear Margaret,

I really need your help. My husband has a four-year-old son from a previous relationship, and I love this boy like my own child. We also have a seven-month-old baby girl. The four-year-old has begun trying to push me out of the house. Every day he tells me to leave and that he doesn't like me any more. He also purposefully breaks my things. My husband and I have custody of him, and his birthmother comes in and out of his life when it's convenient for her. So I guess you could say that I'm the only mother figure in his life.

This hateful behavior just recently started, and we've been together for over two years. As you can see from what I've already said, lately he's become very disrespectful of me and the baby, too. I've caught him trying to hurt her. Needless to say, I've become frightened of him and feel that I can't so much as leave the room for an instant.

Constantly keeping an eye on him is difficult. My husband works 11 P.M. to 7 A.M. and has to sleep during the day, so I feel like I'm the only parent taking care of the two kids. When my husband *is* involved, he treats his son like a baby and lets him get away with murder. I believe that he should be exploring independence and learning how to do things himself without always having someone do things for him, while at the same time learning to obey.

I'm very torn right now. I love my husband and my stepson very much, but I don't know how much more I can take.

Exhausted and Ready to Quit

## *Response*

Dear Exhausted,

I highly recommend a family therapist. There is more than one dynamic causing your stepson to act and react in these ways. Your stepson may be angry at his birthmother for more or less neglecting him, and you're the one on whom he's venting his feelings. Secondly, most four-year-olds do resent the arrival of a new baby. That's behind part of your stepson's behavior. He may see and feel the closeness that exists between you, your husband, and the child you had together. He feels left out and unsure that you'll continue to love him, too. This causes him to be insecure and angry, so he pushes the limits. In order to feel secure he needs both affection and verbal assurance from you and your husband that he is loved.

We hope that your husband can find a few minutes each day before he goes to work to spend some one-on-one time with his son to read a book, play a game, or just goof around. It's preferable that these minutes are spent in interaction, not in passive activities such as watching TV.

Your stepson also needs reasonable boundaries that do not move and that have clear and predetermined consequences. He needs to know exactly what he can and cannot do, and when he crosses a boundary, he needs to know exactly what will happen. This will add to his sense of security.

In order for him to explore that independence you spoke of, your stepson also needs to have choices about some things. Some simple examples would be, "You may wear this or that—pick one." "You may have a snack of an apple or an orange." "When you're done picking up your toys, you may choose between these two TV shows." "Bedtime is in ten minutes. You may look at a book alone or with daddy, which would you like?" We were amazed at the increase in cooperation when we gave our kids simple choices within the nonnegotiable boundaries that we set for them.

Most of all, the boy needs the security of knowing that both his dad and his stepmom who are raising him agree on what is good for him. It's urgent that you come to an agreement on his boundaries. Because you and your husband disagree on how much to expect of your stepson, you could greatly benefit from the guidance of an unbiased third party, like the counselor, who can help you decide together what is appropriate. The fact that you and your husband do not agree increases your stepson's anxiety and insecurity. Try to do the disagreeing behind closed doors, and encourage your husband to support you in front of his son.

You are raising this child, so you must be given the authority to discipline him in a fair and reasonable way throughout the day. But most birthparents we know sometimes do resent the discipline of the stepparent, no matter how loving he or she is. The solution? For the preservation of your marriage, the peace of your home and, ultimately, the well-being of your stepchild, your husband needs to make a conscious decision to let you parent his child. This is another reason the help of an objective third party (the counselor) is needed—someone who could convince your spouse that it's safe to trust his son to you. Your husband must, for your sake and the sake of his son, allow you to be a real mom to both his children.

About the way your stepson treats the baby—try to show him that he's the big brother, that the baby really needs him, and that he is special to her. Show him things he can do to help. Supervise everything, of course, but allow him to touch her and bring things to her and care for her in simple ways. He desperately needs to feel part of the circle of love that includes all of you.

Your exhaustion and sense of helplessness are likely caused, in part, by your just having a new baby. In addition to everything else, you're simply physically tired. Perhaps a friend or relative could lend support so that you can rest. If the therapist thinks it will be good for your stepson, you may want to consider preschool for him a couple of mornings a week. This may give both of you the break you need from each other. Head Start is free if you qualify, and some church funded programs are subsidized so the parents have to pay only a nominal amount.

To sum up, get into family therapy as soon as you can, come to some clear agreement with your husband on discipline and house rules for your stepson, and find a way to take a break and get some rest.

Remember,

> *The testing of your faith develops perseverance. Perseverance must finish its work so that you may be mature and complete, not lacking anything. If any of you lacks wisdom, he should ask God, who gives generously to all without finding fault, and it will be given to him.*
>
> —*James 1:3–5*

And cling to this knowledge:

> *The Lord gives strength to his people;*
> *the Lord blesses his people with peace.*
>
> —*Psalm 29:11*

Please read the next letter for more on this subject.

Margaret

## *Question*

Dear Margaret,

My wife and I have been married only a few months. My three kids, ages eight, ten, and twelve, and her two kids, ages nine and eleven, all live with us. They all leave every other weekend to visit their biological parents. It's the same weekend for them all, so my wife and I have some time alone together. Before my wife and I got married, my kids really liked her and everyone got along. Now it seems like she's hounding my kids all the time. She's always had rules for her kids about doing chores and picking up all the time, while I've always been a real laid-back kind of dad. Now she wants to impose her same rules of living on my kids. Of course, they don't like this one bit! I don't see why they should have to change just because we now all live together. But she won't leave it alone! She wants all the kids to pick up after themselves, and have chores, and so forth.

**In terms of parenting, the parents' job is to prepare their kids for life on their own. One way this is done is by giving age-appropriate responsibilities and jobs within the home.**

All we do now is fight about what's fair. I say, "What's a little mess? Let kids be kids." The only time we have peace between us is when the kids are gone. My kids are starting to resent her, and she's never happy with them. Can you help?

Sad Dad

## *Response*

Dear Dad,

Trying to blend rules and expectations for daily living is one of the biggest challenges of blending. In practical terms, with so many people in the house, you surely can't expect your wife to pick up after everyone. It's simply not possible. And an orderly home (not rigidly so, but orderly) is a home where things can be found when needed. When things are a mess, frustration builds. People are often late for school and work when a home is in disorder and necessary items cannot be found. Professional organizers point out that when you can never find things, you waste money, buying more things to replace what you already have but can't find.

In terms of parenting, the parents' job is to prepare their kids for life on their own. One way this is done is by giving age-appropriate responsibilities and jobs within the home. When you don't expect your kids to clean up after themselves and don't give them chores, how will they become responsible and self-sufficient adults?

Ask yourself, "Is my wife really being too hard? Or am I trying to be the 'good time' dad? Am I so afraid that they won't like me that I let them do whatever they want? Do I want them to become responsible, independent adults, or do I want children who are always dependent upon me and who have little self-discipline?"

If you want your children to be successful as adults, they need to learn life skills. One life skill is respect for those in authority. "Everyone must submit himself to the governing authorities, for there is no authority except that which God has established. . . . Consequently, he who rebels against the authority is rebelling against what God has instituted" (Rom. 13:1–2). What better place for children to learn respect and obedience than with their own stepparent?

Other life skills are cooperation for living in shared space, being responsible for possessions, and self-discipline to see a job through to completion. Your children can't learn these life-skills if you expect nothing from them. Parenting is not a popularity contest, nor is a good parent primarily a pal. *Parenting is a job*—your *job.* And your children's learning to be responsible is part of their job of growing up.

A few years ago the Rev. Walter Wangerin, a former columnist for the magazine *The Lutheran,* wrote a wonderful article on this very subject. He said, "I was willing to sacrifice the love of my son for the sake of my son. I was prepared to suffer his lasting anger, so long as he survived."[4] The story in this inspiring article titled "Sacrificing My Son's Love," ends with his college-age son coming home on vacation and telling his dad how much he loves him. In contrast, we could write a long list of parents who've completely lost their grown children, because their kids learned from an early age to have no respect for their parents, and from childhood learned to live selfish lives.

If you really believe in your heart that your wife is being too hard on your kids and her expectations are too high, then I recommend that you get the insight of an objective third party. We needed such help. When our children entered their teens, we began to question our expectations of them. We wondered how much to control and how much to let go. We found a few visits to a family counselor to be of great benefit.

> *For lack of guidance a nation [family] falls,*
> *but many advisers make victory sure.*
>
> —*Proverbs 11:14*

Here's another passage of Scripture upon which to reflect:

> *"My son, do not make light of the Lord's discipline, and do not lose heart when he rebukes you, because the Lord disciplines those he loves, and he punishes everyone he accepts as his son." Endure hardship as discipline; God is treating you as sons. For what son is not disciplined by his father?*
>
> —*Hebrews 12:5–7*

As you father your children, follow the example of God the Father.

Margaret

## *Question*

Dear Margaret,

My husband and I have been married for three years. The first year was hell because my husband's nineteen-year-old son was living with us. He stayed out all night and slept all day, left filth and messes everywhere, and worked only off and on. Like my husband, I work hard all day and couldn't stand to come home to this lazy slob and his messes—and have him expect me to get dinner on for him, too! When my stepson lived with us, my husband and I fought constantly. Finally, my stepson moved out. Peace reigns. He was forced to get a regular job and move in with some buddies, and our marriage blossomed.

Now he's been in trouble with the law. We're thankful that it's not drugs, but he was in jail for a couple of days and is now on probation. He wants to come back and live with us. (He's still working.) I say—no way! My husband says—he's changed and he needs us.

The very thought of his coming back here to live drives me nuts. I am so desperate, I think that if my husband invites him home, I may leave. I love my husband, and I don't want to leave. But I know from experience that I can't live with this young man.

By the way—since he moved out, my stepson and I have a decent relationship. I know that if he comes back, this will not last.

Feeling Caught Between a Rock and a Hard Place

## *Response*

Dear Caught,

The worst thing you could do for either your marriage or your stepson is to have him come back home to live. We hope your husband is right and that your stepson has changed. But whether or not he has, you are not responsible to make his life work.

You can, however, give help and support to your stepson without having him live in your home. Have him over for a good meal at least once a week—twice if he wants to. Let him talk, and really listen to him. Share your lives with him. Give him a call once in a while and ask

**You can, however, give help and support to your stepson without having him live in your home.**

him how he's doing. If they have compatible schedules, encourage your husband to take his son out for lunch. Open your laundry room to him once in a while if need be.

*Do not give him money. Do give him love, encouragement, and support.* We're glad to hear that you and your stepson now have a good relationship. Tell him that you want to keep it that way, and you know that if he comes back your relationship will be damaged, and that's one of the reasons he can't come back—your relationship with him is too important.

If your husband or you think this advice is not sound, let us tell you that we had to do the same thing with one of our kids. He still has his struggles, but he's making it on his own. He feels so much better about himself than he did when he lived with us and was more dependent. Success breeds an increase in self-confidence, which in turn breeds more success. After two years, that same son landed a career-track job, and we can see that he's going to make it in life. We believe this outcome would not have occurred if we had allowed him to come back home. Sometimes our kids need an extra push to make it into adulthood. Reversing the forward movement and allowing them to come back only retards their forward progress.

For other readers, I'm not saying never to allow your adult children to return home. A person just out of college who needs a few months to get reoriented to the real world, a grown child within a few months before marriage, or a temporarily unemployed kid with a good work history—all may be in the category of those who need to return home temporarily. In these cases, when all are in agreement, it can work out.

For these situations, we suggest drawing up a contract for adult children who live in your home. The contract would list in detail your expectations of your son or daughter, and what he or she can expect from you. Here are some examples of issues to put in writing: Will he be required to share in the expenses of running the household? Which household chores is she responsible for and how frequently will she have to do them? Are visitors of the opposite sex allowed in his private space? Do you allow smoking? Drinking? Do you expect her to go to church? Can he call you to pick him up if he's been drinking? Do you have to cook for her?

All of this—and anything else you believe would be required for peace in your home—should be included in a contract between yourselves and any adult child who wishes to return home. Parents may be able to find some examples of such contracts on the Internet.

Let us pray, every day, that the following psalm will be true of our adult children:

> *Oh, how I love your law!*
> *I meditate on it all day long. . . .*
> *I have kept my feet from every evil path*
> *so that I might obey your word.*
> *I have not departed from your laws,*
> *for you yourself have taught me. . . .*
> *I gain understanding from your precepts;*
> *therefore I hate every wrong path.*
>
> —*Psalm 119:97, 101–102, 104*

Always praying for our children,
Margaret

Chapter 4

# Nurturing Your Marriage Relationship

## *Question*

Dear Margaret,

My wife and I have been married for six months, and this whole blending-family thing is a nightmare. My relationship with her kids (who live with us) was fine before we got married. Now they hate me. They often don't speak to me in my own home. But worse than the way the kids behave is the gulf that's developed between my wife and me. Whenever we disagree about the kids (which is often), we defend our own (I have kids, too, with regular visitation), and then we end up resentful and angry at each other. I can't believe that just a few short months ago we were on our honeymoon and so in love. The last few weeks I've begun to think that I've made a terrible mistake.

We're looking for a counselor, but before we find one, I need to know—is it worth the bother? Should we even try? If our feelings of love are gone, what's the point? I'm so disappointed because we both thought we'd gotten it right this time.

Disappointed and Ready to Quit

## *Response*

Dear Disappointed,

In eight years of stepfamily ministry, almost every remarried couple we've met has at some time questioned the wisdom of their getting married. Even many couples in first marriages experience a questioning stage. When there's a problem or problems that seem insurmountable, the human tendency is to run away from the pain.

**In eight years of stepfamily ministry, almost every remarried couple we've met has at some time questioned the wisdom of their getting married.**

One reason this type of questioning is so prevalent in second marriages is found in your statement, "We thought we got it right this time." When divorce happens, people become acutely aware of the way their ex-spouses fall short of the ideal, fall short of being the ideal mates. Consequently, we go out to look for someone who is "perfect," meaning he or she has those qualities our former spouse lacked.

The new person has the missing qualities, but that person is probably deficient in some things we didn't realize we liked (or at least took for granted) about our first husband or wife. In the pain and anger of divorce, people tend to forget the reasons why they married the first time. The "perfect someone" who has the important missing qualities may not have the ex-spouse's taken-for-granted good things.

When Roger and I began to entertain for the holidays, for example, I became frustrated that Roger wasn't helping me. I went from having two kids to having five, and I needed more help than ever to put on a nice Christmas dinner for our now very large, extended family and guests. And there he sat, doing nothing, or doing his own thing in the garage! It never entered my mind that he didn't know what to do. My first husband and I had never discussed who did what when we entertained. We were just very good at it—a real team. For the most part our roles were unspoken—he just knew what to do, as did I. But now I'm married to a man that in the first year of our marriage had no clue about these things. He was a whiz at fixing cars and could repair anything around the house. I had no idea there was something he simply didn't know how to do!

***Love is a choice you make and a commitment you keep.***

In front of our marriage counselor I was able to state the specific ways that I needed his help. The next time we entertained, he was able to ask me how he could help. I learned also that he needed some advance warning on what I'd like him to do. Now, all these years later, we, too, have become a team and enjoy entertaining. It doesn't look the same as the team in the first marriage, but it's our team. It works, and we enjoy it. To get to this stage in our mature relationship though, we needed commitment, patience, and excellent communication. To achieve excellent communication, we needed the help of a counselor.

We encourage you to get counseling and to hang in there—to choose love. What you're discovering is the reality of love. Love is not just the unrealistic American idea—something you helplessly fall into and out of. It's not just a glowing hot passion for one another; it's not even a warm fuzzy feeling. *Love is a choice you make and a commitment you keep.* If you choose to stay committed, choose to treat one another kindly and thoughtfully, and work to know and understand one another, you'll be rewarded with a long-lasting deep-down fire between you that never goes out. Warm, continuously glowing coals are much more desirable for long-term warmth than hot fire that flares up, burns, and flickers out.

With the help of a stepfamily counselor you'll be able to come to some agreement about the children. You need a coach to help you see that the stepparent may have some good, objective input about the kids. And the birthparent, over time, can learn to trust his or her kids to the stepparent.

Read the letters in the previous chapter about blending kids and discipline. I also encourage you to join a support group where you can receive empathy and encouragement from others in a similar situation. Take heart! The questioning stage you're experiencing is a normal part of the blending process. According to Dick Dunn's book, *New Faces in the Frame,* this stage may be followed by, or perhaps was prefaced by, a crisis and can be followed further by stages of acceptance, growth, and renewed love.[1]

**Instead of thinking "I win" or "she wins," think about how your relationship and your family can be the winners.**

Another thing you can do to decrease the conflict in your home and in your marriage is to change your thinking about conflict resolution. Instead of thinking "I win" or "she wins," think about how your relationship and your family can be the winners. If you can find a way to function as a family and you keep your commitment to one another, you'll get beyond the yo-yo stages of crisis and questioning and move on (probably when the kids are older) to a wonderful stage of reward. How do we know this? We're in that place ourselves! Love is never sweeter than the mature, committed love of the reward stage.

Let our love for one another be as God's love toward us: "I have loved you with an everlasting love; I have drawn you with lovingkindness" (Jer. 31:3). We encourage you to choose kindness and everlasting love, even when you don't feel like it. You'll reap a reward!

> *Let us not become weary in doing good, for at the proper time we will reap a harvest if we do not give up.*
>
> *—Galatians 6:9*

May God bless your marriage and give you hope,
Margaret

## *Question*

Dear Margaret,

My husband and I have been married for six months, and our children take up so much of our time, attention, and emotional strength that there's no time for us. We both have custody and have ex-spouses who only see the kids every other weekend. My ex is not very consistent in his visits, so we often have my kids even when we don't plan on it. This means our plans to be alone are often thwarted. We're always missing dinner together as we drive our kids to various sporting and school activities. When we *are* all together, chaos reigns, because we haven't yet worked out all the family rules, and the kids are still working out their relationships.

Even when all the kids are gone, so much time has passed since we've been together alone, and so much kid stuff needs to be discussed, that we still don't focus on one another. I can't blame my husband for this. We're so busy and so pressured, there are so many issues to resolve and so many decisions to make that we never get around to "us." I'm scared now, because it seems like our love will die if it doesn't get more attention.

My husband says, "Yea, we're pressured and too busy now, but the kids have to come first for now, and they'll grow up and then we'll have time." To be honest, I'm lonely and want to be close to him now. I fear that soon nothing will be left of our relationship.

Other than making more hours in the day, is there a way out of this? Is there a way to still have an intimate emotional relationship even though we're so busy with the kids?

Lonely and Married

Read on.

## *Question*

Dear Margaret

We know couple time is important, but we're just too tired out for it! How can we make time? We know we can't wait until the kids grow up to spend time together!

Timeless

## *Response*

Dear Lonely and Timeless,

The alarm bells are ringing in your hearts for good reason. You're both right—before you know it, the kids will be gone. But the real question is, what kind of relationship will be left between you and your spouse when that time comes? Finding a place in your life now for couple-time is vital, not only to the future of your marriage but to the security and well-being of your children. Your home is not stable and your children are not secure if you don't have a solid marriage around which it all revolves. Notice: Your family and home revolves around your marriage, not around your children!

**Notice: Your family and home revolves around your marriage, not around your children!**

I applaud both of you who wrote for caring so much for your kids. In the early days of remarriage an endless number of things have to be worked out, from family rules to kinds of meals, to how those meals will be eaten. Life goes in every direction now as there are twice the number of children and thus twice the number of activities—all of which consume the hours of your day.

The time has come to get some of this clutter and chaos out of the way. Take a two-pronged approach: saving time and finding time.

First, save time by having a plan. The next time you're alone—or the next time you can shut the door on the kids—sit down together and make a family plan. Based on what kind of family you want to have, decide house rules. Carefully read the previous chapter on discipline. Decide ahead of time what the consequences and rewards will be for both undesirable and desirable behaviors. An amazing amount of time and conflict can be avoided by making an advance plan. Also, you'll probably notice that reducing conflict reduces fatigue levels for all.

**An amazing amount of time and conflict can be avoided by making an advance plan.**

Save time and reduce fatigue, too, by making sure that each person knows what his or her jobs are and what's expected. Divide household chores fairly, and don't make your expectations too high for the abilities of the individual. Make sure neither of you is carrying more of a load than one person can bear—always help and support one another. *And* offer more kudos than complaints for the help you receive.

You may also be able to save time by reducing the number of activities in which each child is involved. Talk to the children separately and see if they'd be willing to give up some of their activities. You may find that they're willing to drop something. Many families have found relief from overly busy schedules by asking their children to choose only one sport or one extracurricular activity per semester. You may discover that kids, too, are happier when less busy! The children, as well as both of you, will be less stressed and will have more time for more important at-home things . . . like homework! Once you've discussed these things alone together as a couple and then alone with each child, have a family meeting. With a united front, tell the children your plans for the family. Immediately begin to act in the way that you have laid out. Included in this plan will be weekly family meetings.

It amazed me how much more efficient our communication (and more fair) when we called a family meeting to lay out a new policy or to make the new schedule. Trying to remember changes, asking or informing each individual in the family about changes is simply too stressful. I'd ask the same kid six times, "Did I tell you we're going to grandma's for Sunday dinner?" while someone else never knew it. Sitting at the table for a family meeting and telling everyone at once works much better.

Also, without family meetings, enforcing a new family policy—such as "If your housework job is not finished by Saturday at noon, you cannot go out with your friends"—will inevitably cause a "You didn't say it that way to me," or "I didn't know! You have to let me go!" If you tell everyone at once you avoid much complaining and cries of "not fair." Family meetings, too, give each child an opportunity to tell you what they think about the latest family plan. Adjustments and changes are constantly needed in order to adapt to an always growing family.

Now that you've *saved* some time, *make* some time for your marriage. The ideal family plan will include a weekly date for you and your spouse, and a monthly getaway without kids. Fortunate is the couple whose children all visit their other parents on the same weekend! It saves lots of money on sitters and expensive weekend getaways. Since we had all of the children all of the time, the only way we could have a getaway was by dividing the children up amongst family and friends for overnights. Once we had a wonderful week when we sent them all to camp at the same time.

You could farm out the children and then stay home alone. Beware: When we tried this, we ended up doing projects and work around the house. Working around the house could be good for your marriage, as long as you actually work *together*. If you can't afford to go away each month, tell your children that the third weekend, or the last weekend, or whatever, is your couple time. Then . . . make sure you take that time for your marriage.

If an unreliable ex-spouse may or may not show up to get the kids on that weekend, then you'll need to have in place a back-up plan. Keep the kids informed. Tell them, "The third week of the month is for us as a couple, and if dad [or mom] doesn't come, you'll be going to ________." Call upon grandparents (who often may feel left out of a blended family) and friends with whom you can exchange favors. Let me emphasize that this back-up plan should be *preplanned!* You don't want your children to feel unwanted. Their looking forward to going to grandma's or their best friend's house overnight if their dad or mom doesn't show, may actually help them feel better, as well as safeguard your precious couple time.

**Commit yourselves to some time alone in which you *don't* allow yourselves to discuss the children or the family plan.**

Some ways to be alone:

- Take a walk together.
- Share a hobby that does not include the kids (museum visiting, concert going, taking a class, skiing, fishing, rock collecting, bird watching—anything!).
- Tell the kids you're having a time-out and sit alone in a room together with a cup of tea, even if it's just for a few minutes.
- Do a ministry at church or a charitable activity together. Examples: work in a soup kitchen one night a month, teach a class together, and so forth. Obviously, avoid things that require too much preparation.

Commit yourselves to some time alone in which you *don't* allow yourselves to discuss the children or the family plan. We made this rule for ourselves, and were shocked to learn that we had nothing to talk about the first few times we went out for dinner! I'd given up so much of my life for the children, they were all I had to talk about. But as we all got used to living together, Roger and I learned to share our innermost thoughts, talk about books that we were reading and ministries that we were planning or sharing in together.

Our time alone soon began to feed on itself. As we spent more time focused on each other, we had more of a life without kids to share with each other. But I'll never forget those dinners when we sat in silence because we'd vowed not talk about the children, and we couldn't think of anything else.

Your fears are justified. Like a plant, love dies if it's not fed and watered. Please keep your love well nourished in the greenhouse of time and commitment.

*For this reason a man will leave his father and mother and be united to his wife, and they will become one flesh.*

*—Genesis 2:24*

*At the beginning of creation God "made them male and female." "For this reason a man will leave his father and mother and be united to his wife, and the two will become one flesh." So they are no longer two, but one. Therefore what God has joined together, let man not separate.*

*—Mark 10:6–9*

May God bless your couple love,
Margaret

Read further for more about the marriage relationship.

## *Question*

Dear Margaret,

Because of the way our first marriages ended, when my wife and I got married we were committed to spending some time alone together each day (a few minutes talking or taking a walk), each week (dinner out), and each month (an overnight getaway). We love doing each of these.

The problem is, one or more of our kids will resent our time alone together and cause any number of hindrances. When we're ready to go on our walk, someone will suddenly be sick or urgently need help with homework. When we're figuring out childcare for the weekend getaways, they throw fits and say they won't go to so-and-so's house. Any ideas on getting the kids to cooperate?

Surprised and Frustrated

## *Response*

Dear Surprised,

It's not unusual that the children may resent your attention to each other. They'd rather have their respective parent all to themselves! They don't really care about your privacy until you teach them, over time, that it's something to care about. Nor do they care about your needs as a couple. If they had their druthers, they'd probably wish for their biological parents to be reunited, as unrealistic as that may be.

When you're getting ready for your daily time alone, make sure each kid is settled first with an activity of his or her own. If the kids get along together, tell them, "This is kids' time. What game would you like to play tonight?" If they're doing homework, get them started first but tell them, "I'll help you for ten minutes, but this is your work, and you're the one who needs to do it." Then go on your walk. In other words, make it seem that they're not being excluded, but are being included in some other activity or responsibility. However, be firm that you're going on the walk.

**As much as possible, use the kids' time with their other biological parents as the time that you go away.**

For your weekend dates or getaways, let the kids help plan where they'll go and how they'll spend their time, again being very positive and firm that you *are* going away. As much as possible, use the kids' time with their other biological parents as the time that you go away. This way, the kids will be going to something—not being left out of something. If they don't have visitation with another parent, make meaningful plans for them. For example, maybe they'll go to the skateboard park with friends or out to a movie with grandma and grandpa.

*Don't give any indication that your going is optional.* If the kids are continually belligerent and actually hostile, they may have some unresolved issues from the divorce or remarriage, and may need to work it out with a counselor. But if you make your kids feel that what they're planning to do is important, they'll likely feel less left out, consequently, less concerned about your going.

Moreover, your kids' accepting your couple time helps them accept that you are, indeed, now married to each other. It's an adjustment. Teach them that you've learned some lessons about marriage, and one thing you're going to do right this time is have couple time. Eventually, they'll come to understand not only what you're doing, but will also learn what it takes to make a marriage work—even their own some day.

> *What God has joined together, let no man [no one, not even kids] separate.*
>
> —*Mark 10:9* (NASB)

> *Children obey your parents in the Lord, for this is right.*
>
> —*Ephesians 6:1*

> *Join with others in following my example, brothers, and take note of those who live according to the pattern we gave you.*
>
> —*Philippians 3:17*

God bless your couple love,
Margaret

Chapter 5

# Conflict Resolution and Communication

## *Question*

Dear Margaret,

My husband and I don't consider ourselves combative people, but ever since we got married and all moved in together (I have three kids; he has two) we keep fighting. We knew it would be tough because of the kids, and many of our arguments are about the kids. What are some tips on how to have a difference of opinion without it escalating into an argument? Do you have any suggestions?

We are simply fighting too much.

Fighting and Hating It

## *Response*

Dear Fighting,

First, when you have a disagreement, keep in mind the intended outcome. Rather than thinking about which one of you will win this argument, decide that you want your marriage and your family to be the winners of every disagreement.

**Decide that you want your marriage and your family to be the winners of every disagreement. Eliminating the need to be the personal winner will reduce the need to be defensive.**

Eliminating the need to be the personal winner will reduce the need to be defensive. When someone disagrees with us, it's natural to defend ourselves, or often, our children. When in a disagreement, take some deep breaths before answering and try not to use defensive language. Instead of automatically defending yourself, try some active listening response. Say, "I see" or repeat back to the person what you understand him or her to be saying, or simply nod your head. All these help the speaker know that you're really hearing what he or she has to say.

Listen with respect. No heavy sighs, eye rolling, or any sarcastic body language. (Even if you have to hold yourself very still!) When you're feeling irritated, hurt, and defensive, it's difficult to listen in this way, but practice will make perfect!

When you realize that you are far too emotional on an issue to maintain this kind of control, you may need to take a "time out." Ask your spouse to stop the discussion. Doing so can seem scary to the person who has the issue that needs to be resolved, so you have to assure your partner that you're only taking a break. In our case, we then make a commitment to talk about it "in two hours" or "tomorrow after work." When some friends of ours call for a break, one of them goes for a walk while the other sits in the walk-in closet. When the one spouse returns from the walk, the other comes out of the closet.

Then, with their emotions under control, they can resume their discussion.

Over time, Roger and I have gotten better at listening to one another and fighting fairly. We learned, however, in order to avoid one or the other of us blowing up, *some subjects are always off-limits*. No one is allowed to say, "You're just like your mother!" or "I bet your previous spouse had the same issue with you!" That's not to say one of you is allowed to let an issue to go unresolved by just saying it's off limits; but certain hurtful comments and reminders of already forgiven hurts are not helpful in solving current problems. Other things that are off limits in fair fighting are name calling, saying "you always" and "you never," and dragging other people into your personal conflicts.

**Certain hurtful comments and reminders of already forgiven hurts are not helpful in solving current problems.**

Some couples dialog better about their problems when they write them down first and, then, sitting close enough to touch, read the clearly articulated issues to their spouses.

Good, on-going communication means keeping short accounts: deal with disagreements and hurts early before they explode into an emotional outburst. And when you disagree over the children, don't contradict one another in front of them. As we've said before, present a united front to them. Decide your policies behind closed doors and then come to your kids as a supportive couple in a parenting partnership.

> *A gentle answer turns away wrath,*
> *but a harsh word stirs up anger.*
> *The tongue of the wise commends knowledge,*
> *but the mouth of the fool gushes folly.*
>
> —*Proverbs 15:1–2*

We hope these ideas help you communicate more and fight less.

May the Lord bless your growing communication skills,
Margaret

Chapter 6

# Help in Blending—Good Counsel

## *Question*

Dear Margaret,

You frequently recommend counseling, but when we went to our church for help, nobody understood the problems related to stepparenting. I then went alone to a private therapist, and that experience wasn't helpful, either. We don't want to give up on this marriage, but the pressure the kids place on our relationship is going to break us if we don't find some applicable help soon! How do we find a counselor that really understands blended families?

We are,
Desperate for Help

## *Response*

Dear Desperate,

Finding a competent stepfamily therapist can be tough. And to make it more complicated, we found that a social worker who was very effective with one of our daughters couldn't get another daughter to open up. Not every counselor is right for each family or each person. But we know from experience that counseling can make all the difference. We applaud you for not giving up and are glad you're still searching for the right kind of help.

You can begin your search by going to the web site for the Stepfamily Association (look under "Resources" at the end of this book). They maintain a directory of family therapists who have taken the Association's training. If none is near you, call a family therapy group in your area and ask them what, if any, kind of training they've had in blended-family issues. Inquire if their counseling is based upon a Christian worldview, and what resources and books they'd recommend for stepparents.

At a meeting I polled a group of fifteen counselors, asking how many had received training specifically aimed at helping stepfamilies. Only two mentioned one class period spent on the subject, the rest had none. So finding a therapist who understands stepfamilies may take some searching. But if you ask the above questions, and if the counselors *do* have a good resource list and *have* taken any extra time to educate themselves, you should be able to get help.

***The fear of the Lord is the beginning of knowledge, but fools despise wisdom and discipline.***

***—Proverbs 1:7***

Ron Deal, a licensed family therapist and a speaker and writer on stepfamily issues, says, "A good follow-up question to ask is, 'How might you treat a stepfamily differently than a biological family?' You are not looking for any specific answer here; you simply want to know if they can tell you the difference."[1] A family therapist qualified to help stepfamilies, says Ron, should be able to give you several examples of how a stepfamily is different.

*Pray for guidance and keep looking for help!* We found it, and we know you can too. But remember,

> *The fear of the LORD is the beginning of knowledge,*
> *but fools despise wisdom and discipline.*
>
> —*Proverbs 1:7*

> *Trust in the LORD with all your heart*
> *and lean not on your own understanding;*
> *in all your ways acknowledge him,*
> *and he will make your paths straight.*
>
> —*Proverbs 3:5–6*

God bless your search for help, and may it really help,
Margaret

## *Question*

Dear Margaret,

My wife has been going to a counselor she really likes. I must admit, the way she relates to my kids has improved. Now though, she wants me to go too, because the counselor suggested that I come. I don't want to! My wife has probably been telling this guy all my faults, and if I go I feel as if I'm going to get ganged up on. I wouldn't mind getting the help, but I don't need to be criticized! I get enough of that from my wife. Besides, what if the counselor wants to get into my childhood? I really don't need to dig up all that stuff. What would you do?

Skeptical

## *Response*

Dear Skeptical,

I see what you mean. Nobody wants to feel ganged up on; and since your wife has a history with this therapist, I can see why you'd be worried about it, but going to counseling isn't like that. A good family therapist is skilled in seeing both sides of the story. Even now, as he's asked to see you, he's trying to understand your perspective. In fact, you could go to a session alone with the intention of telling your side of things. You may be surprised how much it will help.

Don't worry about the counselor discussing anything you don't want to talk about. Therapists don't try to dig into things from the past that we don't want to share; the issues of the here and now will be enough to deal with. As you begin to have a trust relationship with the therapist, you may decide to reveal more, but the agenda for discussion is set by you and your wife, not by the counselor.

**Not only can a good therapist see both sides of the story, he or she can help you and your wife understand one another.**

By going to therapy with your wife you'll both be learning the same things, which should help considerably in creating the united front you need to successfully raise your children. A stepfamily counselor can be a wonderful unbiased third party when it comes to helping you establish objective boundaries with the children, and great at helping you think of appropriate consequences for breaching those boundaries. And best of all, not only can a good therapist see both sides of the story, he or she can help you and your wife understand one another. This is probably the best benefit of all. By all means—go!

*Be not wise in your own eyes;*
*fear the Lord and shun evil.*

*This will bring health to your body*
*and nourishment to your bones.*

—*Proverbs 3:7–8*

*Get wisdom, get understanding; . . .*
*Do not forsake wisdom, and she will protect you;*
*love her, and she will watch over you.*
*Wisdom is supreme, therefore get wisdom.*
*Though it cost all you have, get understanding.*

—*Proverbs 4:5–7*

May you grow in wisdom and understanding,
Margaret

Chapter 7

# Blending Holidays and Traditions

## *Question*

Dear Margaret,

During our first Christmas as a blended family, my wife and I were on our honeymoon, so the kids were with their other birthparents, and we didn't have to deal with holiday logistics. We just gave a gift to each child when we got back.

Now we're starting to think about our first Christmas together, and I tell you, I'd rather not! It's so complicated—what with all the grandpas and grandmas, and working around visitation schedules and everything. I want to just forget it and let them do whatever they want with their other parents. The few ideas I've brought up were immediately shot down by the kids.

Give me one good reason why we should even bother to celebrate anything!

I'm feeling a lot like—
Scrooge

Please continue reading, Scrooge.

## *Question*

Dear Margaret,

It seems like my kids are never here for birthdays, Mother's Day, and the like. What can I do? I either feel mean and angry, demanding a change in visitation so they can be with me, or I feel sad and lonely because they aren't here! Any ideas?

I am,
Ambivalent

Please continue reading, Ambivalent.

## *Question*

Dear Margaret,

My wife's people are big on parties, and I never have been. Why should we celebrate birthdays, anyway? And aren't Valentine's Day and Mother's Day just hyped by advertisers so businesses can make big money? What's the big deal? Give me one good reason why we should pay attention to any of this materialistic stuff.

Just sign me,
Skeptical

## *Response*

Dear Scrooge, Ambivalent, and Skeptical,

Well! This is one of my favorite subjects. I'll give you lots more than one reason why you should celebrate holidays and establish traditions in your blended family. But I do understand that blending traditions can be an emotional issue.

**Blending traditions can be an emotional issue.**

The reasons we do things, and why certain things have become a tradition in the first place, usually have little, if anything, to do with logic and everything to do with emotion. So traditions (things you always do in the same way to celebrate something) are emotional by definition. Therefore, giving them up or changing them can bring out the worst in people.

For two years we argued about when to open Christmas gifts. Rog's family always opened them on Christmas Eve, and Margaret's family always got up bright and early and opened them on Christmas Day.

I would say, "Why not read the Christmas story on Christmas Eve, since traditionally that was when baby Jesus was born? And then celebrate on Christmas by opening our gifts, because we celebrated His birth last night?"

Roger would say, "We should open them on Christmas Eve, in anticipation of His coming, because after all, Christmas Day is a religious holiday—that's when we go to church!"

"Well," said Margaret, "I never went to church on Christmas in my life! And the only services in our town were on Christmas Eve!"

Our church actually solved this conflict for us when it began its own new tradition—one year we had Christmas Eve services, and the next year we had Christmas morning services. So our family alternated—along with the church—and the decision made for us. Peace at last!

This all changed, of course, when our kids grew up and became themselves part of a couple. It's been a miracle that so far our in-law children open gifts with their parents on Christmas Eve, so we still have Christmas Day. But we can see the year rapidly approaching when we'll have to do as our parents have done and celebrate on a day not even Christmas—so that all our children can be with us to celebrate the Lord's birth.

"Why," you may ask, "go through all this hassle?" Why not just ignore holidays and observances as one of the writers above suggested?

*Why We Need Traditions*

Holidays and traditions serve several good purposes. First, our awesome God commanded His people to observe certain days. So in the Old Testament, special days, ceremonies, and traditions became important to God's people. In Numbers 29, for example, God tells Moses to have the people take a day off from work, all get together, blow trumpets, party like crazy, and make tons of racket! This feast of the trumpets, as it was called, was in preparation for making offerings to God.

God gave Moses the plans and the procedures to use in worship, sacrifice, and remembrance of His faithfulness to them. God also commanded His people to build up a pile of rocks near the Jordan River. Whenever the children would ask, "What are those rocks for?" the Israelites told their kids about God's faithfulness in getting His people safely across the river when pursued by the enemy. Rocks are totally meaningless things—unless the telling of a story gives them meaning. Then they become a powerful symbol. In a similar way, we can use the material items of various holidays to remember the Lord and His faithfulness to us.

**Traditions usually don't happen unless you make a point of creating them, and you and your family are the only ones who can give them meaning.**

Queen Esther did this when she created the holiday of Purim. Her heart was full of praise to God for saving His people from annihilation, so she instituted a holiday to remember it. On this day the Hebrew people feast, exchange gifts of food, and give to the poor as a way of remembering the gift of life they were given by God. From these examples, and many more, I argue that God gave His people traditions and symbols as a way of remembering His faithfulness to them.

### *Celebrate the Lord's Faithfulness*

How has God been faithful to your family? It was He who brought you together. How can you celebrate His doing that? Please give it some thought. Traditions usually don't happen unless you make a point of creating them, and you and your family are the only ones who can give them meaning. In our culture, any and all holidays could become nothing more than a reason to spend money. *But we each decide what the meaning of these special days will be for our family.*

In our family, we celebrate God's faithfulness in bringing us together by eating together and remembering the first night the children met. We remember this day by always having the same food and, after all these years, the same centerpiece. We talk about the first night we were ever together, and how the children felt about meeting one another. It's interesting to see what each one recalls; everyone remembers something different. The important thing *is to remember it together*—and *to give God the glory for what He has done for our family.*

***Knowing that on certain occasions they can count on certain things to happen makes the family secure.***

### *Celebrate the Family*

Doing the same things year after year not only helps us to remember God's faithfulness to our family, but tradition also helps create a family identity. It makes a child more secure when he or she can say, "In our family we always ___________"; "At my dad's house for Christmas we ___________"; and, "At my mom's house we always ___________ for Easter." *It matters more that you do something to remember important days, and matters less what that something is. Knowing that on certain occasions they can count on certain things to happen makes the family secure.*

An old story tells about a Jewish boy who insisted to his mom that he wanted to stop being Jewish. Their family was not very religious, and since the boy was only seven years old, his mother couldn't imagine why he'd say this. When she questioned him more closely she discovered that he felt left out of the fun that surrounded the celebration of Christmas. He didn't go see Santa; he didn't get to sing carols; he didn't get presents, except just one on Hanukkah. He told his mom, "Being Jewish is just about all the stuff I don't get to do."

That got his mom motivated. She spoke to her husband and they got involved in their local synagogue. They became careful to observe the Sabbath in the traditional Old Testament way, with bread and candles and prescribed prayers for various members of the family. She talked to her Rabbi, and she read about many Jewish holidays and customs. Together, with other Jewish moms in their area, the boy's family began to organize celebrations that other families could share.

As the family became more observant of Jewish tradition, and as the boy's mom and dad explained the symbols and meanings of their religion to their son, he became excited about being Jewish. He enjoyed his Jewish identity. Becoming more observant gave him not only the ceremony and tradition his young heart longed for, it strengthened their family identity and bound them together with others in their community. Now, instead of feeling that being Jewish left him out of some things, he felt it gave him an identity and made him feel that he belonged. With the use of tradition, we can give meaning to our family holidays and reap the same benefits.

For ideas on how your family can create special and meaningful holidays, sit down with the kids and stepkids, and find out what's important to them. You may be surprised! My husband thought that our kids were too old for certain things, but found out, when we skipped doing them, that those things had become important symbols of our family identity. The kids still wanted to do them—these events had become part of who we were as a young family.

For example, I wanted to eliminate Christmas stockings this year, but the kids (all adults!) made it clear that they still wanted them. I'd made the boys' stockings for them when they were really little, taking months to sew on each piece of felt and tiny sequin by hand. And shortly after Roger and I were first married, I had wooden shoes made for the girls and painted by a country painter. When I told them I was out of ideas about what to put into the stockings and shoes, *they* gave me ideas. Using these symbols as part of our Christmas celebration is obviously important to our adult children.

When you listen to the children, also hear who they mention. Is it important for them to visit Aunt Louise *and* Grandma Jones? Or would one visit on that side of the family be enough? If you can't fit all the important people into the holiday season, try to make arrangements for the children to be with those people for something special at another time.

When we blended our family, we retained the families of our former spouses, and all four of our own grandmothers were alive. This gave our children seven grandmothers! Every December we'd have a Christmas party every Saturday, as well as on one or two other days of the month. In addition, we'd visit a special aunt and uncle who I visited each New Year's Day since childhood.

**One thing that is *not* important is the day upon which you actually celebrate.**

How could I possibly continue to do this? I couldn't. So I made up a holiday. In the month of October I'd have "Apple Sunday." On this day, I'd invite my aunt and uncle and their grown children for dinner. I'd use a bright red tablecloth and place a silver bowl of shiny apples in the middle. Everything served for the meal had something to do with apples: pork loin basted with cider, or ham with apple glaze; yams baked with apples; grandmother's famous apple salad; apple muffins, apple cake, and apple pie. We observed the Apple Sunday "holiday" for several years.

### *Pick a Day*

So by all means, if on a given holiday you can't be with certain people whom you love—or who are important to your children—make up your own holiday. Include the people who are important to your children in some kind of tradition to which you bring meaning.

It's a way to maintain bonds, make those extended family members feel like part of your lives, and keep your children aware of the greater family of which they are a part.

One thing that is *not* important is the day upon which you actually celebrate. What day in December will you be together? Make that be your Christmas Day. Were your kids grown up when you got married? You may want to have two completely separate Christmas celebrations. Don't force your grown children to celebrate Christmas with one another just because you're married. Celebrate birthdays when you can, and celebrate Mother's Day and Father's Day on the Sunday that's your turn to have the kids. The important thing is to actually have the celebration, and do it for your family in a way that's meaningful to them, and that includes some things that are always the same.

### *Pick a Tradition*

As with the first writer above, establishing new traditions as a blended family can be challenging and painful, especially when one's ideas are rejected. But as I've said, it's important to your family identity to have celebrations and traditions. It's sometimes difficult to convince the kids, especially teenagers, to participate. Bring them into the planning as much as possible. Have a family meeting, and ask the kids what's important to them in the celebration of this holiday. Ahead of time, give the children specific parts, to which each agrees, in the day's activity. If, for example, you're planning a Christmas observance, ask the kids if one of them would like to read the Christmas story or prepare a certain food. Ask them what kind of foods they'd like, and then always have the same foods on that holiday. If you have a really cool idea, ask them to try your idea just once and see how it goes. If it works, keep doing it; if it doesn't, have the strength to let it go.

**Try to find that delicate balance between what's required and allowing free choice.**

A group of people asked me to plan a celebration for them, then they criticized every idea I brought to them. When I thought it out, I realized that I was "telling" them my ideas without asking them what they had in mind. So I called each one individually and asked his or her thoughts. None had a clear idea of what he or she wanted. But because I asked, and listened, and made them feel that their feelings counted in what I'd developed, their attitudes changed and they became willing to participate and go along with what I chose. The evaluations at the end were generally favorable, and if I plan it again, I have some ideas from their feedback on how to improve the activity. Although this wasn't a celebration in my blended family, I thought the lessons I learned were important in getting teenagers in stepfamilies to participate.

So listen to the children, but then again, don't listen to the children! That is, get their ideas, listen to their feelings. But if teens are involved, don't let their hormonally critical attitudes make you give up and do nothing at all!

**If you and your husband are going to be alone on the actual day of Christmas, or Thanksgiving, or whatever holiday, plan ahead on how to fill your day with meaning.**

Just a word about when teenagers don't want to go to grandma's house or Great Uncle Jerome's for an extended family gathering. When Roger and I first married we had seven grandmothers and a superabundance of relatives in general. As our kids reached their teens, they were sometimes less than enthusiastic about attending extended family events with these numerous relatives.

We taught them from day one (as we sat making valentines for all our grandmas) that it was important to honor their grandmothers and other family members; but we also assured them that after high school they could choose whether or not to attend an extended family gathering.

It's interesting that no matter how they'd fussed and fumed when younger, each of them, after taking perhaps one holiday off, continued to attend most extended family get-togethers. When people say how unusual it is that our grown children want to be with their relatives, I encourage parents to try to find that delicate balance between what's required and allowing free choice.

### *When the Kids Aren't There*

If you and your husband are going to be alone on the actual day of Christmas, or Thanksgiving, or whatever holiday, plan ahead on how to fill your day with meaning.We had a couple in our support group that planned a fabulous Christmas Eve celebration with their blended family; it was wonderful. Then they took the kids to their other parents. In the morning, they found themselves alone with nothing to do on Christmas. They were in tears most of the day. What a wonderful time it would have been for them to take a ski-holiday, go work at a soup kitchen, or visit a more distant relative they couldn't otherwise fit into the schedule . . . if only they'd planned ahead.

### *Celebrate the Individual*

I can't remember the last time we celebrated a birthday on the actual day of the person's birth. Yet we know that it's important for each person in our home to be celebrated as the unique individual and gift of God who they are—so we remember birthdays whenever we can get together.

In a blended family, celebrating birthdays is especially important because, with the second marriage, most of the children have lost their places in birth order. My oldest son, for example, became the second oldest child, and my youngest son moved to the middle, a place he had to share with a stepsister the same age. This shift in family position can hurt a child's self-concept. Because of this displacement, it's especially important to validate the individual child's identity and worth. By remembering birthdays and other special days for the individual, we remind each how important he or she is to us their parents, and to their brothers and sisters.

When Roger and I were first married, the children were young and to them birthdays seemed far apart. So we created "kid of honor" dinners to observe a kid's particular accomplishment. The child being honored would get to pick the food for dinner and select the plates to use. (After all—we had blended dishes.) We sang "she/he's a jolly good fellow" and talked about the game that child had just won, the A he or she received, or the play in which that child had been given a role. One time we honored a kid just for making it through a class he thought he was going to fail! At first, the kid of honor day involved a small gift. Then, as the children got older, the day involved just the special food and dishes and singing the honor song. Finally, when the kids became teenagers and birthdays were celebrated in bigger and more special ways, and they were old enough to "see" from one birthday to another, we dropped the kid-of-honor thing. But it had served its purpose—that of making the individual child feel special as a valued member of our family.

### *Christmas*

When it comes to Christmas, we especially need to remember why Jesus came. Cut down or cut out the gifts if you'd like. You decide how materialistic to make it, but don't stop celebrating the coming of the Messiah! After all, He came to "save his people from their sins" (Matt. 1:21), and that truly should be the biggest celebration of them all.

Remember that Queen Esther and the Old Testament Jews used gift giving for holidays as a symbol of the gift of life. Anything you do—from decorating and lighting a tree to exchanging gifts—can become an object lesson for God's grace and love to us if we choose to give it meaning.

Some simple ways to make Christmas Day a real celebration is to eat together around a special table. You can use candles, perhaps an advent wreath (which you've been using for weeks along with Scripture) or some other candles that represent Christ—the light of the world. By always using the same tablecloth, or certain special plates, or by always serving the same food, you've created a tradition in much the same way as God's people, the Hebrews, obeyed the biblically commanded feast days with the required ceremony and utensils that God prescribed. You can read about these in the books of the Law in the Old Testament.

Use Scripture or, if your children are young, Bible story books to keep in mind the true meaning of Christ's coming to earth. Every Christmas Day celebration should include a reading of the Christmas story. Have the children read it or tell it in their own words. We've started a new tradition of reading Luke 2 in unison. And remember to pray and give thanks to God for what He has done for your family, as well as simply praise Him for who He is—*the Savior of His people.*

For ideas on how to make your holidays meaningful, many Christian books on the market can help you. One that I've enjoyed is *Let's Make a Memory* by Gloria Gaither and Shirley Dobson.[1]

### *Thanksgiving*

Most Americans celebrate Thanksgiving with a wonderful feast and time with family. In many homes, before eating, family members take turns around the table telling what they have been thankful for in the past year.

All of this is wonderful, and Thanksgiving can become one of the most important holidays if we take time to make it that way. It's been said by some that Thanksgiving is the most truly Christian holiday because instead of being focused on things, the day is simply about being thankful. It's a day we set aside to thank God for all that He is and all that He has done for us.

In the early years of my first marriage, we worshiped at a small Bible chapel. Each Sunday we celebrated the Lord's Supper. One of the elders at the church loved to remind us that we had not come just to thank God for what He had done, but we had come to thank Him for who He is. We can do this with our families on Thanksgiving Day by simply thinking about the nature of God. Who is He? Celebrate the very nature of God! Your Thanksgiving will be so rich.

Here are just a few characteristics of God and some verses you can read to celebrate him. God as Creator: Genesis 1. God as Father and Leader: Jeremiah 31:9. God as Comforter: Zephaniah 3:7. God as Healer: Exodus 15:26; Is. 53:4–6. The God who keeps promises: 2 Chronicles 7:14. The God who saves: Psalm 80:7; John 3:16.

You can learn about the nature of God in: Deuteronomy 6:4; Jonah 4:2 and John 17:1–3.

For His natural attributes and many other things about the nature of God, use a topical Bible or a biblical cyclopedic index. There are also many paperback Bible studies such as those from Kregel Publications and NavPress that discuss the nature of God. You can use small parts of any of these to find a verse or two to read to your family as you remember together all God is and all He has done.

### *Easter*

Easter is the most high and holy Christian holiday, the day when we remember that our Lord Jesus Christ was raised from the dead. Easter stands in huge contrast to Good Friday, the most somber day, a day when we recall the price of our sins. Easter, on the other hand, is to be a day of great joy and celebration. Remember the apostle Paul said, "And if Christ has not been raised, our preaching is useless and so is your faith" (1 Cor. 15:14). *Wow!* If not for the Resurrection, if not for Easter, our faith would be entirely useless. This calls for big time celebrating!

Our culture has gone in for glorifying the symbols of spring on Easter day—from Easter bunnies and eggs (symbols of fertility and new life) to new clothes and cute hats (symbols of new lives and a fresh start). None of these things are wrong in and of themselves. But what's important is how we think of the day and how we lead our children to celebrate. Do we give it a spiritual meaning? Or do we just "go with the flow" and do whatever?

Not being raised in a liturgical church, I was an adult before I became acquainted with Lent and all of its powerful symbolism. When I learned of these things, I realized that this season can be a most meaningful time with the family. During the weeks before Easter, we can spend our family devotion times contemplating what Jesus gave up when He came to earth. By giving up something for Lent, even if it's one small thing, we can recall the sacrifices of our Savior, who left the splendor of heaven to become a poor Hebrew boy and a suffering Messiah. Throughout these weeks we can read Scripture passages with our families about His life and prophecies of His death. All of this culminates in Good Friday, the day we quietly recall the horror and pain of the cross.

I loved the way the first church we attended as a blended family remembered the Lord on Good Friday. The congregation had the Lord's Supper and read, throughout the service, verses from the day of the Crucifixion. As the death of the Lord came closer in the reading, the lights were more and more dimmed until, as we read about the hour of His death, all lights were extinguished, the last candle was carried out, and the congregation left in darkness and silence.

Then comes Easter!

When we returned to church on Easter morning, the sanctuary was ablaze with spring flowers and bright lights. We joyfully sang, "Christ the Lord Is Risen Today! Alleluia!"

And we carried this wonderful celebration on into our home. We'd sat all month around a centerpiece of spikes, a handmade crown of thorns, a glass of colored water ("wine"), and bread, reading many Scripture passages regarding Christ's betrayal and death.

And on Easter we celebrated His resurrection! You may choose to spend this day with extended family or just your own family. You may use, as we do, a special pastel cloth and a traditional centerpiece with lots of newly awakened spring flowers. On Easter you may celebrate with Easter eggs, whether the secular ones (symbols of new life) or the ones found in Christian bookstores, filled with Scripture promises and reminders from God's Word. Or you can decide to do none of these rather ordinary things. But whatever you do—*celebrate the risen Lord!* Because as the apostle said, "If he has not risen, our faith is in vain."

> **We create and celebrate holidays and traditions then, as a way to remember God's faithfulness to us as a family, and as a way to create a family identity.**

As we teach our children the meaning of this day of joy unspeakable, we can use any and all symbols that are helpful teaching aids. If it is something that will help us remember Christ's death and resurrection, if it will help us recall God's faithfulness to us, especially if it will help us remember His faithfulness in saving us from our sins, then we have found a good tradition for our family Easter celebration.

### *Celebrate Your Love*

We create and celebrate holidays and traditions then, as a way to remember God's faithfulness to us as a family, and as a way to create a family identity. And as with the birthdays, we find ways to celebrate the individual. In addition, it's vitally important to celebrate your love. I contest the idea that Father's Day, Mother's Day, and Valentine's Day are worthless materialistic dates on the calendar.

#### *Valentine's Day*

What love is more fragile than a second love? What husband or wife is more insecure than one who knows he or she is the second one? Who could be more insecure than a woman or man whose first marriage ended because of the infidelity of his or her spouse? In a second marriage, there is so much pressure to be Mr. or Mrs. Perfect—yet none of us are. All of us fail at times to do or say the loving thing. We try to forgive and move on, yet how can we be sure that we're still loved? What better day than Valentine's Day to show our love and commitment to one another?

What if you're not a romantic person? What if you never know what to say? Instead of thinking, *Hallmark wallet raid!* you could think, *Hallmark to the rescue!* Of the billions of Valentine cards, one will speak with your voice and express your sentiment. *Take the time to find it.*

If you can't find the words to say how you feel about your spouse, you, more than anyone, need to find that Valentine that says it for you. If you're uncomfortable with romance, take advantage of the excuse of Valentine's Day to give a gift or do a thing that shows your spouse you really do cherish him or her.

My husband is not romantic. But he makes a decision, year after year, to find the perfect Valentine card especially appropriate to us, and many times he's moved me to tears by this token of his love.

*Mother's Day/Father's Day*

Stepparents are often rejected by stepchildren for whom they do so much. Stepparents have no legal rights, yet give of their time and of themselves to care for another's child. Other than a child's birthparent, who, more than a stepparent, deserves be honored on Mother's Day or Father's Day? But if a kid is still rejecting his or her stepparent, who's going to do the honoring? Who's going to teach these children to respect, honor, and appreciate their stepparents if not the birthparent?

**Teaching our kids to honor their stepparents is just plain good parenting. By teaching our kids to respect and honor their stepparents, we're preparing them to love and honor their spouses.**

Dads out there—I beg you—honor your wife on Mother's Day. If you don't like cards and flowers and eating out, then find some way to honor her that seems right to you. *But don't skip it!* Moms out there, what better way to start teaching your child to respect his or her stepdad than by helping them find the right Father's Day card?

Teaching our kids to honor their stepparents is just plain good parenting. By teaching our kids to respect and honor their stepparents, we're preparing them to love and honor their spouses.

Are you convinced yet that holidays and traditions are worth the trouble? Read on.

## *Question*

Dear Margaret,

I know that you teach other stepparents, and I wanted to share with you how we have Mother's Day at our house. I hope you can use my story. The first Mother's Day we were together was very traumatic for my husband and his children, for it was on this day, two years before, that his first wife died. I thought it was reasonable for him to have another year to grieve and work it out. Because our communication was good in those first couple of years, I told him that by the second year, I'd expect a real Mother's Day.

He didn't disappoint. For our second Mother's Day together, he bought me a corsage with six roses, one for each of the children in our blended family. The kids cooked breakfast and he cooked dinner. We all sat together in church. He took our pictures. It was wonderful.

The next year . . . nothing! We went to his mom's for dinner. Period. I bought her a plant. I got nothing.

I was cut to the core and then furious. The kids were still little. If he didn't take them shopping to buy me a card or gift, who would? Who'd teach them? I put them all into the car, took them to a grocery store, gave them $5.00 each, and told them to buy something for me for Mother's Day. At this point, it wasn't as if I was going to feel honored—I just wanted them to learn to do what was right.

Later that day, a dear old saint "saved" us from our conflict. At evening church she asked me how my Mother's Day had been. I told her the truth. I got teary. "I gave up a good career," I said, "to stay home with his kids! With only a couple of kids, I could handle working outside the home. But not with six! For all practical purposes, I *am* their mother! I'm the one who takes them to the doctor, takes care of them when they're sick, rocks them when they're sad, and prays with them every day. Why is he not thanking me for raising his children? Why does he not appreciate me and my hard work?"

This dear, sainted woman, an old friend of my husband's family, had experience with a thoughtless son. She told me, "I had to give my son a good talking to about how he ignored his wife on Mother's Day, so I think I'll have a talk with your husband, too." Wisely, she didn't do it that day. But a fine warm day a few weeks later, she asked him to accompany her to her car, which she had parked far away in the parking lot. Of course he did. To this day, I don't know what she said to him, but since then he's never neglected me on Mother's Day. The children are older now and, one by one, as they have their own money, they make Mother's Day an opportunity to show their love and appreciation to me.

**Your spouse deserves to be honored for what he or she does and for who he or she is in your child's life.**

Please teach the couples in your group to honor their spouses on Mother's Day and Father's Day. As the children learn to follow their parent's example, it can make all the difference in how the children treat their stepparents. These holidays are also great opportunities to show your spouse how you really appreciate all that he or she does for the children.

Just sign me,
A Grateful Stepmom

## *Response*

Dear Grateful,

What could I add to that? Even if your spouse's involvement in your children's lives is not as extensive as is the mom who wrote above, your spouse deserves to be honored for what he or she does and for who he or she is in your child's life. Teach by your example how to do that.

Here is some encouragement from God's Word:

> *The Lord said to Moses, "Speak to the Israelites and say to them: 'These are my appointed feasts, the appointed feasts of the Lord, which you are to proclaim as sacred assemblies.'"*
>
> —*Leviticus 23:1–2*

> *Mordecai recorded these events, and he sent letters to all the Jews throughout the provinces of King Xerxes, near and far, to have them celebrate annually the fourteenth and fifteenth days of the month of Adar as the time when the Jews got relief from their enemies, and as the month when their sorrow was turned into joy and their mourn-*

*ing into a day of celebration. He wrote them to observe the days as days of feasting and joy and giving presents of food to one another and gifts to the poor. . . . The Jews took it upon themselves to establish the custom that they and their descendants and all who join them should without fail observe these two days every year, in the way prescribed. . . . So Queen Esther, daughter of Abihail, along with Mordecai the Jew, wrote with full authority to confirm this second letter concerning Purim.*

*—Esther 9:20–22, 27, 29*

*Train up a child in the way he should go: and when he is old, he will not depart from it.*

*—Proverbs 22:6* KJV

*One [person] considers one day more sacred than another. . . . Each one should be fully convinced in his own mind. He who regards one day as special, does so to the Lord.*

*—Romans 14:5–6*

*Therefore, brethren, stand fast, and hold the traditions which ye have been taught, whether by word, or our epistle.*

*—2 Thessalonians 2:15* KJV

What follows the Leviticus passage above in the Bible are the details of *seven* special days of celebration prescribed by the Lord God for His people. All of these special days, scattered throughout the year, helped them remember God's faithfulness and drew them close together as a people and close to Him. We in blended families can use our holidays and traditions to do likewise.

May God bless your holidays as you fill them with Him,
Margaret

Chapter 8

# Blending Kids, Blending Space

## *Question*

Dear Margaret,

I'd hoped that when I remarried we'd be a family, but our kids don't get along! They resent being made to do things together. They hate sharing rooms. I'm afraid the day is coming when my birthkids won't want to visit me because they don't like my stepkids. Help—before it's too late!

Frustrated and Worried

Please continue reading for your answer.

## *Question*

Dear Margaret,

My husband has done a good job of teaching his preteen children to be respectful of me as their stepmother. But when they come to visit, they and my kids are always at odds! It seems as if we can do nothing together as a family because the kids all hate each other! How can we reduce the fighting amongst the children?

Frazzled Stepmom

## *Response*

Dear Frustrated and Frazzled,

First of all, think practically. You're a blended family and that's what you will always be. You're not going to turn into the Brady Bunch! Many emotions are creating issues for your new family. It's important to remember, though, that when your children have visitation with you, they've come to see you, not to spend time with your stepkids. But you do, of course, want the members of your family to all get along. Following are some of the sources of blended-family conflicts and what to do about them.

### *Parents Need Some Separate Time with Birthkids*

Our family social worker told us that kids in blended families complain most to her about not getting to spend enough time with their non-custodial birthparents. Your children may have some resentment because their own birthparent lives with other kids now, kids who get to see you all the time. When birthkids come for a visit, begin by spending time alone with them. Take them out to breakfast or dinner. Really share yourself, your feelings, and your ideas. Listen intently while they talk about school, about their friends. (Do *not* let them complain about their custodial parent.) If you can't afford to go out to eat each time, explain to your spouse and stepkids that you need an hour alone with your kids, tossing a ball, going for a walk, playing a game. After your one-on-one time is up, take steps to integrate your children into your blended family.

**Having predetermined consequences will go a long way in reducing stepsibling rivalry and helping things go more smoothly between all of you.**

The experts say not to force birthchildren and stepchildren to do things together. But you can, together with your spouse, focus on making visitation time as family-like as possible. That means that your birthchildren are not treated as guests in your home, but as part of the family. Sit down and eat your other meals together around the table—all of you. Make a point of letting each person talk and really listen to one another.

### *Chores and Family Rules Help the Blending*

Believe it or not, giving chores to the visiting kids will contribute to helping them feel like members of the family rather than like guests in your home. Along with your resident kids, have your visiting kids help set the table, make their beds, or feed a pet. Make sure to compliment all the kids on good attitudes and jobs well done. These types of jobs and responsibilities are not optional but are required of all children.

As discussed in the chapter about discipline, having the same rules, standards, and expectations for all the kids, and having predetermined consequences will go a long way in reducing stepsibling rivalry and helping things go more smoothly between all of you. Each kid will likely push the limits a few times in order to find out if the boundaries really are secure. It's vitally important for all of the children, and the parents too, to know what the limits are and what will happen when those limits are violated.

As parents, we then don't have to rely upon how we feel at the moment or make a decision in the heat of a crisis because we already know what the situation warrants. And we aren't adding confusion and insecurity to the situation, because the kids know and understand the house rules.

It makes everyone more secure and less competitive to have house rules that are reasonable and fair for all.

### *Start Small*

After a time, try some *short* all-family activities, like watching a video (parent's choice to reduce conflict), go to a movie together, rake the leaves together, or go hiking. (The last one was big in our family and really made us feel bonded, especially after we got lost a couple of times!) Make these activities brief at first, and increase them in length and complexity as the children get used to being together. If older kids refuse to do even brief activities together, give them more time, reward them for going if they do go, give them a chance to give you feedback afterward. If your kids are already in their teens when you marry, there may always be a limit on what you can do as a "family." Just remind yourself again that your kids are coming to see you, and they need you to parent them whether they like your new family or not.

**Just remind yourself again that your kids are coming to see you, and they need you to parent them whether they like your new family or not.**

### *Sharing Space*

Allowing each child to have his or her own private space will go a long way in reducing stepsibling rivalry. The resident children may feel invaded each time the stepsiblings visit, and the stepsiblings may feel as if they have no place to call their own. Ideally, each kid should have his or her own room. Of course, in larger families this may be impossible, so make sure each kid at least has a bathroom drawer or shelf, and a bedroom drawer that is just for that kid and totally off-limits to anyone else. A plastic under-the-bed storage box may be useful for the visiting child's personal things. Have a predetermined consequence for anyone who violates another's space or another's property.

We knew a blended family with mostly teens, who made five bedrooms in the basement. The rooms were not spacious, but each child had his or her own bed, dresser, closet, and nightstand, and most especially, a door that could be closed. Remember, right from the start, have house rules that include the way the children's space will be used such as no visitors of the opposite sex in any bedroom and not entering someone else's room without knocking.

You as parents also have stuff no one can touch. Mom, if you share your makeup with your birthdaughters, expect to share it with your stepdaughters. Be consistent. Dads, you decide if kids can use your tools and what the conditions are for using them. In blended families, we all have to give a bit, letting more people than we'd like use our things and come into our private spaces. But remember, the kids will someday grow up! This whole space and property issue is one we *really* enjoy not dealing with as we now live in a wonderfully empty nest.

*Neutral Territory*

Just as it is important for each child to have his or her own space, it is important for children to learn to live in shared spaces. Family rooms, sound systems, and computers may all have to be shared. Although some toys are special, and no one else can touch them, other things are for all to share. With these shared items, we had "ten-minute trade-offs" over whatever they argued about, such as shared toys, a swing, or the trampoline. As the kids got older, this was especially important with video games. It's important to set a time limit with these, because a kid can play one game all day, taking it from level to level. Trade-off time may have to be a bit longer, but make sure you choose a reasonable amount of time and enforce the taking-turns rule. Sharing and taking turns is an important life skill. Encourage your kids to choose games that several kids can play together.

**Many experts say it's good to let the kids work out as many of their own conflicts as possible.**

### *Let the Kids Work It Out*

Kids need to learn how to negotiate and relate on their own. Many experts say it's good to let the kids work out as many of their own conflicts as possible. The house rules will give them a start and some guidelines, but kids need to work out their own relationships.

There may be occasions, for the sake of sanity and/or safety, when you have to intervene. When the kids begin to bicker, try to make a quick decision about which arguments are petty and which are dangerous. If the kids are arguing about the TV remote, remind them of the family policy of ten-minute trade-offs. If they're arguing over who gets the chair, let them figure it out for themselves. If they're in a physical fight, it, of course, must be stopped at once, and your predetermined consequences for such behavior immediately enacted. With very young children you may have to do actual teaching about sharing, and so forth, just as you would with any siblings, but when the inevitable petty conflicts arise, try to let the kids solve their own problems.

**Kids need to know that your marriage will last and that they *don't* have the power to break it up.**

### *Give It Time*

Compromise is of course the key to resolving any conflict, and kids learn this as they go through life. But compromise can be a scary thing to a kid who's jockeying for position in a new family. In order for children to feel safe enough to risk compromising with a stepsibling, they need to know that this relationship is permanent. One marriage has ended, either by death or divorce. Kids need to know that your marriage will last and that they *don't* have the power to break it up. If they can be sure of the permanence of this home, they'll be more secure and allow themselves the vulnerability required for compromise.

The ages of the children you're trying to blend makes a huge difference in how well blended you will actually become. But no matter what their ages, time is your strongest ally. It takes time for a family to form, time for the kids to build relationships, and time for them to work out their problems with each other. The children may not become best friends, but they should be able to learn to live together with mutual respect.

May you go to God for the wisdom that you need to blend your family. As time passes, and you share a life, the kids will feel more comfortable with one another, and you will blend more and more.

> *But the wisdom that comes from heaven is first of all pure; then peace-loving, considerate, submissive, full of mercy and good fruit, impartial and sincere. Peacemakers who sow in peace raise a harvest of righteousness.*
> —*James 3:17–18*

God bless your blending!
Margaret

## *Question*

Dear Margaret,

I'm so freaked out I don't know what to do! I think my teenage daughter and my husband's teenage son are interested in each other! Right now, she lives with us, and he lives with his mom. But he comes for regular visits and is talking about spending all next summer here. I'm in a panic. My husband says cool it—as soon as they live together they'll despise one another in the typical sibling way.

I'm not so sure. What do you think?

Worried

**Have very clear house rules: no one of the opposite sex visits in the other's bedroom.**

## *Response*

Dear Worried,

> ***"You will keep in perfect peace him whose mind is steadfast, because he trusts in you."***
> ***—Isaiah 26:3***

Your situation is not uncommon. Biologically speaking, your kids are just two teenagers who are being thrown together a lot. Apply the usual rules of good parenting for teens—don't leave them alone in the house together, just as you would not allow any teens to entertain the opposite sex while you are gone.

Have very clear house rules: no one of the opposite sex visits in the other's bedroom. Make sure there's a lock on the bathroom door to prevent inadvertent voyeurism.

Talk to each of them separately about your concerns. If they know you're aware and watching, they'll have to be careful about their relationship. On the other hand, if they think you're "freaked out," they may act out a little more just to "pull your chain."

We noticed that our upper elementary son and daughter related to one another sort of like boyfriend and girlfriend while we were dating. This stopped instantly when we got married. Then they became huge competitors, getting into the worst fights in the family as they vied for the position of oldest kid. In high school their friends sometimes teased them about the possibility that they could marry each other, and they were totally grossed out. As adults, they are married to other people and are wonderful friends.

We have a hunch your husband is right, but it'll take time. In the meantime, protect them. For more peaceful thinking, make a mental note to yourself that when they're old enough, it's not legally wrong for them to date, because in reality they're not related.

Be careful and beware, but you can also be calm. As the prophet Isaiah said,

> *"You will keep in perfect peace him whose mind is steadfast, because he trusts in you."*
>
> *—Isaiah 26:3*

May God's Spirit protect you and your family,
Margaret

## *Question*

Dear Margaret,

I'm feeling sad and experiencing an unexpected sense of loss that I hadn't anticipated. Our children were only three and five when we divorced. My husband's leaving came as a complete surprise to me. Right up until the week he left, on late mornings, like Saturday and Sunday, the kids would come into our bed and cuddle with us. This was always such a special time, and my children and I still share these kinds of moments with me alone.

My ex-husband is remarried, and our children came home very sad from visitation last week. The oldest one, my daughter, was even teary. It seems that when the children attempted to go into their father and stepmother's bed on Saturday morning they found themselves locked out of the room. Their dad told them no kids were allowed in the bedroom. His new wife also has children who live with them: two girls, ages ten and thirteen, and an eight-year-old boy. They're not allowed in the bedroom either.

Is the rejection of my children from the family bed really necessary? My kids are still so young! What do you think?

I am,
Sad for My Kids' Loss

## *Response*

Dear Sad,

We understand that it's difficult when you must leave a cherished and wonderful family tradition behind, but we do agree with your ex-husband. While it may be okay for a preschooler to snuggle in this way, alas, your little son is the only child this young. Your ex-husband and his new wife probably have found that the rules in this matter need to be the same for all the children. If some could come into the bed and snuggle, and some could not, the rejection for those who could not would be too great. Her children are certainly too old to snuggle in bed with a man who is not their biological father. Imagine yourself remarried. Would you want your daughter in bed with another man? Of course not. The end of the family bed is a sad reality for divorced families.

**The end of the family bed is a sad reality for divorced families.**

If you have good communication with your ex, you may talk with him about the children feeling sad so he can make a point to hold them and cuddle with them at other times.

Talk to your children. Assure them that it's okay to feel sad about not being able to crawl in bed with daddy anymore, but it's really not okay for them to be in bed with someone that is not biologically related to them. We hope you can have this discussion without sounding angry against your children's dad and stepmom. Since the divorce was not your idea, this loss was also not your decision, but it has happened. Like the divorce itself, all you can do is accept it as graciously as you can and comfort your children.

> *"I am the Lord, who heals you."*
>
> —*Exodus 15:26*

*"He heals the broken in heart and binds up their wounds."*
*—Psalm 147:3*

May God bless you, and keep you, and heal you,
Margaret

## Chapter 9

# A Blended House

### *Question*

Dear Margaret,

I really love my home. It's been a comfort and a sanctuary to me and my kids since my husband's death. Now I'm engaged to be married to a man who has a couple of his own kids. If we finish off the basement, we'll have enough rooms for each kid to either have his or her own room or to share one with a brother or sister with whom they already share.

But my fiancé is against living here. He wants us to buy a house together. The kids change their minds every other day, so they can't help us break the stalemate. What do you think we should do?

Home Lover

## *Response*

Dear Home Lover,

We always recommend that, if financially possible, couples move to neutral territory when they remarry. We give many reasons for this.

1. Living so closely with the past may hinder the development of the new family. Many memories are connected to your home, memories of a previous family and a family life that you no longer have, which sometimes you will still grieve. Do you want your new husband and new family to live with these shadows of your past? Doing so makes it hard in the present, setting up a competition that doesn't have to exist.
2. Staying in your home while others move in will probably give you and your children a sense of being invaded and of having some of your rights taken away. When I and my rambunctious boys moved into Roger's house, the boys swooped down on the playhouse in the backyard, shooting imaginary guns out through the windows and hooting and hollering all kinds of wars sounds. My oldest stepdaughter ran into the house sobbing, "It's my playhouse! It is, it is! It's not a star-fighter! They can't play with my playhouse this way!" It was more difficult to share what belonged exclusively to her and her sisters than it would have been had we moved to a new house and built a playhouse that belonged to all of the children from the start.

   **Staying in your home while others move in will probably give you and your children a sense of being invaded.**

   Another stepdaughter came home from school and discovered that her stepmother had ripped all the wallpaper off the bathroom wall. "What are you doing to my house?" she wailed. It would have been easier emotionally if they'd all moved to a new place for a new start and decorated it together.

3. No house is perfect. As your new spouse or his children find things about your house that are impractical or not quite right in some way, and they complain or want to change it, you may feel like it's a personal assault. Your beloved home has been criticized.
4. Space conflicts and issues over what's yours and what's his will be magnified many times if you stay in this house. It's bad enough choosing which microwave to keep and which one to give up without having to defend your home turf, too.
5. When his kids make messes and don't pick up as promptly or as well as your kids, you may feel like your home is being compromised. If you move to a neutral territory, it will belong to all of you, and the motivation to take care of the space you share will be far more equalized.
6. Think of your former spouse's extended family members. It may be difficult and even painful for them to see someone new residing in the place their loved one once called home. Imagine being in their shoes. Would it not add insult to injury for you to see a newcomer take over not only your loved one's family, but also their home?

If one of you has been living in a wonderfully adequate home alone, never having been there with the previous spouse, then, of course, living there will create far less emotional conflict than the examples above. The sense of being invaded, however, and having to give up rights of space and property can still be a problem. We don't recommend it.

Remarrying is not the same thing as becoming a new creation in Christ, yet the following verses seem to apply, reminding us of the principles for a new start:

> *Neither do men pour new wine into old wineskins. If they do, the skins will burst, the wine will run out and the wineskins will be ruined. No, they pour new wine into new wineskins, and both are preserved.*
>
> —*Matthew 9:17*

> *But one thing I do: Forgetting what is behind and straining toward what is ahead, I press on toward the goal to win the prize for which God has called me heavenward in Christ Jesus.*
>
> —*Philippians 3:13–14*

May God bless your blended home,
Margaret

## Chapter 10

# Loyalty Issues

### Left Out Stepparents

*Question*

Dear Margaret,

I'm so sick of feeling left out! Both my husband and I have custody of our kids. Mine are young, but his are teens. They're forever making plans and never informing me until it's too late for me to be included. The other night, for example, just before bed, my husband's high-school daughter came to him and asked him if we were going to her honors breakfast in the morning. As usual, I sat there with a blank look on my face, having no clue what she was talking about. If I were to go to this event it would mean getting my kids to daycare early—something I could not easily do!

I felt hurt and angry that for at least the one-hundredth time, I'd be left out. Yet they act like they *do* want me to come. And I do so much want to be part of this important event! Why don't the kids keep me informed? Or even worse, why doesn't my husband keep me filled in on the important things that are upcoming in their lives?

Just sign me,
Left Out and Hurting

## *Response*

Dear Left Out,

This is a very common problem. Stepparents often feel left out of the circle of love that exists between a birthparent and his or her children. Your husband and his kids had already developed the way they communicate before you came along. They probably don't intend for you to be left out, but without thinking they continue to relate to one another in their old way, the way they communicated before you were there.

To make matters worse, dads are not commonly the ones in charge of the social calendar, which means that your husband probably doesn't pay much attention to things when they're mentioned in advance and relies on his daughter for these last minute updates. He probably always has. So when he doesn't inform you in advance, he's not intentionally keeping anything from you—he, himself, just isn't thinking about it.

**Every family that functions well must have good communication, but in a blended family, it's even more vital and more complicated.**

*Try this:* Have weekly family meetings. Once a week, probably after a meal at which you're all together, talk about upcoming events. Go over the week's calendar and talk about what arrangements need to be made and who needs to be where when. Write everything down on a master family calendar.

Every family that functions well must have good communication, but in a blended family, it's even more vital and more complicated. Most experts advocate the family meeting as an excellent way to improve communication and unity in the blended family.

For information on how to hold family meetings, check out the web site for the Stepfamily Association of America, or the book *New Faces in the Frame* written by Dick Dunn[1] (see "Resources" at the end of this book).

> *Trust in the* Lord *with all your heart*
> *and lean not on your own understanding;*
> *in all your ways acknowledge him,*
> *and he will make your paths straight.*
>
> —*Proverbs 3:5–6*

God bless your blending,
Margaret

## *Question*

Dear Margaret,

I'm engaged to marry a man with one young daughter. I have no children. Whenever his daughter comes, I'm totally ignored and left out. Even if they include me in the outing, they ignore me during the activity. The other day for example, I was so looking forward to our day at the beach, but when we got there, they ran ahead of me to the water, leaving me to look after our things. When I joined them, they continued to talk only to one another and pretty much just ignored me. I find this behavior hurtful and rude.

How can I make my fiancé understand how much they're hurting me? What are some specific things we can all do to make our time together better?

Betrayed

## *Response*

Dear Betrayed,

You feel hurt and betrayed because the behavior of your fiancé and his daughter are hurtful and rude. But chances are, they're relating to one another in the way that they've always related and, in doing so, are hurting you, perhaps without even knowing it. Give them the benefit of this doubt. Do tell them how you feel. Use a word picture if necessary: "When you treat me like this, I feel like ____________." Create a picture that will help to describe your feelings, a picture that both he and his daughter would relate to.

You ask for some steps to take. One thing you can do is work on your individual relationship with your stepdaughter-to-be by spending some one-on-one time with her yourself. Since you're both female, the typical ideas of shopping, lunch, makeovers, and hair salons should provide plenty of activity for just you girls.

Remember, though, his daughter is coming for visitation to spend time with him. Allow him to do so. Tell your fiancé that you understand that he needs time alone with his daughter and give him, say, an hour or two each day, or certain visits that are intentionally just for the two of them. Then tell him that because you expect to become a family, you want to start acting like one now. If you're going to be married, that means that you're an equal partner, not a separate person that he fits into his life on the side. Check out the chapter on blending kids. Your fiancé and his daughter need time alone together, but you need family time, too. His daughter is old enough to sit down and have a conversation about this. She's old enough to hear your feelings about how you feel when the three of you play a game or go to the beach, and she only looks at her dad and never talks

**Cildren are actually most secure in homes where the parents have a strong and affectionate relationship.**

to you. She can be taught how to include you and how to treat you with respect.

Your fiancé needs to know that his daughter is, in many ways, competing with you. She wants her dad all to herself, and she'll make him feel guilty when he shares his focus with you or includes you in their circle of love. Why, you may ask, would an innocent little child do such a thing? Well, she's used to having her dad all to herself, and she doesn't want to share him! She is, as all human creatures are, selfish and self-centered. It's her dad's job to teach her to be otherwise. *She'll stop leaving you out when he demands it and shows her how to do something different.*

The Bible teaches that the marriage relationship has first priority. Remember the vows that say, "Leaving all others and cleaving only onto thee." We've learned in our studies of families that children are actually most secure in homes where the parents have a strong and affectionate relationship. That includes stepfamilies. If your fiancé's child sees that, yes, her parent's first marriage ended, but her parent is now capable of having a strong and committed marriage to someone, it will make the child more secure in the present. As she gets older, it will give her hope for her own marriage some day.

We can't emphasize enough the importance of making the marriage a priority. When I did a survey of thirty stepkids, from ages six to fifty-six, the kids who felt loved and secure were the ones who felt that their parent and stepparent had a good relationship. *A solid marriage relationship made the home solid and secure for the child.*

If your fiancé is not willing to make your relationship first, then reexamine whether you want to marry. We have a friend who expressed the same frustration. The man she dated always put his daughter first and fit our friend in around the edges of his "free time" when he was not with his daughter. She did marry him, and to this day, ten years later, she feels left out and devalued as a person. They've received copious amounts of counseling, but he and his daughter have chosen to not include this dear woman, his wife, in the circle of their love.

You need to discover now if your fiancé is willing to change the way he relates to you when he's with his daughter. Because you're engaged, how you're acting now is practice for when you're married. If he's not willing to make his marriage relationship number one, then you need to decide if this is the kind of life you want to live.

Margaret

Please read on.

## *Question*

Dear Margaret,

My husband is a kind and loving man. But when his children come, they have no respect for me. They turn only to him for help with everything, and won't let me help when I offer. I feel so left out.

Sometimes they smirk at things I say, and they always say, "I don't have to," when I ask them to do such simple things as wash their hands or hang up their coats. My husband is distressed to see this, too, and tells them not to talk that way. But we need more specific guidelines on how to change this situation. Neither one of us seems to know what to do about it. We've only been married a few weeks and want to stop this before it becomes a huge problem.

I Get No Respect

## *Response*

Dear No Respect,

According to a book we've often used in our support groups, *New Faces in the Frame* by Dick Dunn, the stepparent often feels left out. The one person who can help get rid of this feeling, and thereby help everyone feel united, is the birthparent. Dunn tells the story of Gerald and Jane in this book. At a stepfamily support meeting, someone suggested that Gerald build up Jane's position in the family. He began to praise her—give her credit for wonderful cooking, compliment her for how she decorated a room, tell her over and over what a difference she was making in their home—all in front of the children. When a decision had to be made or permission given, the dad said, "I have to talk it over with Jane." When Jane asked a child to do something, Gerald began to reinforce to the children that they obey her.[2]

**A family contract . . . promises the stepchildren that the stepparent will treat them with kindness and respect and also states that the children will be respectful in language and obedient in behavior.**

Moreover, they did things as a family, and Gerald and Jane together made plans and policies. Jane's opinion was valued by the dad and, eventually, by the children as well. Once, something came up and Jane was willing to give permission for a son to go out, but Gerald was hesitant. He made sure that he told his son that he had reservations about letting him go but would do so because Jane thought it would be okay. The child yelled, "Whoopee!" and hugged Jane. She was his hero for the day. This story concludes by the writer saying, "The children's attitude toward Jane did not change quickly, but it did improve over time. Gradually, Jane felt accepted and more and more a part of the family."[3]

Another thing that often increases respectful behavior is to write a family contract. Such a contract promises the stepchildren that the stepparent will treat them with kindness and respect and also states that the children will be respectful in language and obedient in behavior. Everyone signs it. Everyone knows what the consequences of sassing and disobeying are . . . before they happen. Search online under "stepfamily contracts" for ideas.

> *A new command I give you: Love one another. As I have loved you, so you must love one another. By this all men*

> *will know that you are my disciples, if you love one another.*
>
> —*John 13:34–35*

May your love grow as your families blend,
Margaret

## Still Loyal to Ex-wife

### *Question*

Dear Margaret,

My husband thinks that it's still his responsibility to do home and car repairs for his ex-wife. They lived in that house together and that's the car they bought together. They have shared custody of the children, and when he left her, he continued to take care of these things for her.

It's been more than three years since their divorce, and he's been married to me for several months, but he continues to do these things for her. He feels responsible and thinks that by doing those things, he's taking care of his family.

Sometimes I feel as if he has two wives! He says I'm being petty, and as long as everything in our home is taken care of first, why should I care? He says he loves me more than he ever loved her, and I should quit worrying about it. But it just doesn't seem right to me. How can I get him to see that now his loyalty belongs to me and he should not "take care of" things for her any longer?

Second Wife

## *Response*

Dear Second,

For the answer to your question, I called upon two other second wives who are friends of mine: Mara and Linda. This is what they said.

We want to assure you that if your husband says he's loyal and faithful to you, in his heart he probably is. But you're right—now the time has come that he should no longer do these things for his ex. He probably has some guilt over leaving. It's possible that there really should not have been a divorce in the first place, and he knows that. Out of his guilt, he still feels obligated. There was a divorce, however, and he did marry you. Now his loyalties should belong to you. When your husband and his ex got divorced, for whatever reason, their obligations to one another as husband and wife ended. But, of course, the obligation to the children did not end, and this makes his sense of loyalty confused.

**When your husband and his ex got divorced, for whatever reason, their obligations to one another as husband and wife ended.**

You feel bad about his fixing things for her because each time he goes there, you feel as if he's choosing her over you—and in a sense, he is. What is a marriage anyway? It seems as if he's simply changed bed-partners while still being married to his first wife, and that she's getting the privileges of marriage without the responsibilities of maintaining a relationship.

You asked how you could explain it to him. Here are two things to try. First (calmly, not angrily, not sarcastically), ask him this: "Would it be okay with you if I went over to my ex-husband's house and cleaned? How about if I fixed him a few meals?" (This will only work, of course, if these were your usual jobs in that marriage.) If he thinks that's okay (which he probably won't!), ask him to imagine this

**One should always be kind to one's ex and work together with her or him in the best interest of the children.**

scenario: He's taken a new job. The new company sells the same products as the old and is, in fact, a competitor in the marketplace. He took the new job because the pay and benefits were much better. Still, he didn't hate the old job. So, periodically, he goes back to the old company and works a few hours. How would this go down with his new boss? Perhaps these two examples will help him to understand why he's no longer the one responsible to take care of his former home, former car, and former wife.

Linda pointed out to us that his behavior is an example for the children too. While it hurts them very much that their dad and mom are no longer married, they need to see what that means. They need to see that he's loyal to the woman to whom he is now married. Yes, one should always be kind to one's ex and work together with her or him in the best interest of the children. But your husband's loyalties now belong to you—his wife.

Ask him to think about this verse:

> *No one can serve two masters. Either he will hate the one and love the other, or he will be devoted to the one and despise the other. You cannot serve both God and Money.*
>
> —*Matthew 6:24*

May God protect your heart as you bond and blend,
Margaret

## *Question*

Dear Margaret,

Even though it's been two years since our divorce, my ex-husband is still badmouthing me to the children. Every time they come home, they tell me all the bad stuff he said about me, most of which is not true. I feel like I'm always defending myself. I've called him up and yelled at him many times, and he won't stop doing it. How can I get him to stop? In the meantime, what can I tell my children?

Frustrated and Fuming

## *Response*

Dear Fuming,

You absolutely cannot control what your ex-husband does and says. How to get him to stop? You may be surprised at how simple the answer is: Stop listening! What do you tell your children? Tell them that you've come to understand that speaking badly about their dad is not healthy for them or for you, and you're no longer going to do it. You also need to tell them that you're sorry their dad is still so angry with you, but you really can't listen to his criticism anymore. You'd like the pain to stop, so you're asking them that from now on, they not tell you anything their dad says about you.

***Being a loving, consistent mom who is there for [your children] and living a righteous life before them is all the testimonial they need in order to know what kind of person you really are.***

They may share about their day and what activities they did, but you'll stop listening and walk away if they start to talk about the things he said about you. And, of course, you'll not ask them. *Don't worry about defending yourself to your children. Being a loving, consistent mom who is there for them and living a righteous life before them is all the testimonial they need in order to know what kind of person you really are.*

So stop listening. Do this promptly. Do this firmly. Do not waver. It may be the hardest thing you've ever done, but you must do it. Your ex-husband and you are keeping the anger and pain of your failed marriage alive far too long, and it's not healthy for either you or your children. Such anger feeds upon hateful words, your anger feeding his anger, and his feeding yours. Someone has to stop the cycle. Let it be you. You can stop it now, and you need to stop it now, for your own well being, but especially for the well being of your children.

Remember the example of Jesus Himself. When wrongfully accused, He remained silent:

> *When he was accused by the chief priests and the elders [for things of which he was not guilty], he gave no answer. Then Pilate asked him, "Don't you hear the testimony they are bringing against you?" But Jesus made no reply, not even to a single charge—to the great amazement of the governor.*
>
> —*Matthew 27:12–14*

Ask God to help you be like His Son. He will give you the power to remain silent, and to prove who you are by your deeds:

> *Live such good lives among the pagans that, though they accuse you of doing wrong, they may see your good deeds and glorify God.*
>
> —*1 Peter 2:12*

Be a light for your children as Jesus told His disciples to be:

> *You are the light of the world. A city on a hill cannot be hidden. Neither do people light a lamp and put it under a bowl. Instead they put it on its stand, and it gives light to everyone in the house. In the same way, let your light shine before [all people], that they may see your good deeds and praise your Father in heaven.*
>
> *—Matthew 5:14–16*

Be a light in your family,
Margaret

## *Question*

Dear Margaret,

My husband has a sixteen-year-old daughter who's really giving her parents a hard time. The divorce has been over for more than two years, but when we got married a few months ago, she really took it hard. Now she's running with a group of wild friends, has taken up smoking and drinking, and may be using soft drugs. She lives with her mother, and her mother is at her wits end. Consequently, she calls upon my husband several nights a week to help her deal with their daughter.

I can understand that his daughter needs him to be involved in her life, but he's running over there two and three times a week to talk to her, discipline her, and support his ex. I can't take it anymore! He's always choosing them over me! And his daughter never stops the things she's doing. She's acting up so much, that I fear we'll never have any peace. Help! I want my husband with me, not with them! Am I terrible to feel this way?

Neglected New Wife

## *Response*

Dear Neglected,

Your stepdaughter's behavior is not that unusual. Whether or not she's conscious of it, she wants her parents back together and you out of the picture. She's seen, from experience, that if she acts up her dad will come home—so, of course, she does this as often as she can.

***She needs the security of knowing that she's not the one in control of her parents' behavior.***

It's obvious that he needs to stop the cycle. He should be able to set boundaries and consequences for his daughter's behavior without running to their home to do it. He should be able to talk to his daughter at your own home and not have to go there to communicate with her.

If he feels trapped in this cycle of self-defeating behavior, he may need a professional counselor to help break him out of it. He needs to tell his daughter that he shouldn't be coming to her mom's house and that his life is with you now. *She needs to see him be loyal to you. They need to stop allowing her to control them by her behavior, and she needs the security of knowing that she's not the one in control of her parents' behavior.*

In order for your marriage to survive, it must be a priority in the lives of you and your husband. Again, we encourage you to seek a counselor who may be better able than you alone to help your husband see and understand this.

> *Now to him who is able to do immeasurably more than all we ask or imagine, according to his power that is at work within us, to him be glory in the church and in Christ Jesus throughout all generations, for ever and ever! Amen.*
>
> —*Ephesians 3:20–21*

Margaret

## To Whom Should the Children Be Loyal?

### *Question*

Dear Margaret,

How can I make my children understand that their dad is not a good parent? It seems like no matter how many times my ex stands up his children for visitation or how many times he doesn't pay child support, they still love him and continue to reject their new dad. How can I get them to transfer their loyalty to my new husband? I just want a united family.

Looking for Loyal Kids

### *Response*

Dear Looking,

"Do not let not any unwholesome talk come out of your mouths, but only what is helpful for building others up"(Eph. 4:29). Whenever you say bad things to your kids about their dad, you're tearing them down. No matter what he's like, you hurt your kids to the core when you speak against their dad, and you cause huge loyalty conflicts within them. When you quit criticizing their father, they will no longer have to defend him.

**No matter what he's like, you hurt your kids to the core when you speak against their dad, and you cause huge loyalty conflicts within them.**

Remember, your new husband, as important and wonderful as he is, is not your children's birthdad. Loyalty to their stepdad will come only over time as they see the way he treats you and them, and how faithful and true he is to all of you.

They need both their birthfather and their stepdad in their lives. They need their birthdad, because without him in their lives, they'll feel a greater sense of grief and loss. Without him in their lives, their grief and anger about the divorce will take longer to go away—if it ever does.

You can't, of course, make their dad show up, any more than you can force him to be consistent about his child support. But as much as you can, support his visitation time. Encourage him to come, because they need his interest in order to feel secure and valued. Without letting him control or disrupt your lives, be flexible whenever you can about when he can see the kids. *Make sure you're not preventing his relationship with them by your criticism.* When he doesn't show up, do not criticize. Your kids are having a hard enough time when their father breaks his dates with them. Try to imagine how hurt and lost they feel, and don't add to those feelings with your anger and criticism.

**Pray for your ex-husband every day that he will be faithful to your kids.**

> *Get rid of all bitterness, rage and anger, brawling and slander, along with every form of malice. Be kind and compassionate to one another, forgiving each other, just as in Christ God forgave you.*
>
> —*Ephesians 4:31–32*

Pray for your ex-husband every day that he will be faithful to your kids. Encourage (but don't pressure) them to tell him how they feel when he doesn't show up.

> *Then Peter came to Jesus and asked, "Lord, how many times shall I forgive my brother when he sins against me? Up to seven times?" Jesus answered, "I tell you, not seven times, but seventy-seven times."*
>
> —*Matthew 18:21–22*

May God fill your home with peace and love,
Margaret

## *Further Response*

To all of those who wrote on the subject of loyalty issues, I would like to share with you what some professionals have to say about divorce, remarriage, and loyalty conflicts.

**Clinging to the emotional ties of the past, especially negative ones, will rob you, your current mate, and your blended family of the emotional energy and focus that all of you need in order to successfully blend.**

In the book *Positive Discipline for Your Stepfamily,* the authors Nelsen, Erwin, and Glenn state that a divorce is not really final until each person involved has divorced themselves emotionally from the previous relationship. They say, "You have not yet achieved an emotional divorce if the answer to any of these questions is yes."[4]

1. Are you uncomfortable seeing your former partner?
2. Do you have difficulty talking calmly to him or her?
3. Does your former spouse still make you angry?
4. Do you want revenge and try to make friends and family choose sides?
5. Do you think of your ex-partner often?
6. Does your former spouse still enter your home as if he or she belongs there?
7. Do you look for similarities and differences between your former and current mate?
8. Do you have difficulty talking calmly with your current partner about your former partner?
9. Do you have difficulty accepting your former mate's new relationships?

If the answer to any of these is yes, you need to make peace with the past and let it go. Being unable to do this on your own is a good reason to seek professional help. Clinging to the emotional ties of the past, especially negative ones, will rob you, your current mate, and your blended family of the emotional energy and focus that all of you need in order to successfully blend.

## Loyal to In-laws

### *Question*

Dear Margaret,

When my husband left me for another woman, I was devastated and so were his parents. My in-laws and I have always been close, and they, along with my own family, supported me both emotionally and financially until all the details of our divorce and child support could be worked out, and until I got a job.

I'm engaged to be remarried, and my former in-laws are glad for me. I don't want to leave these precious people out of my life. I especially don't want my children's time with them to be limited to when they spend every other weekend with their dad. But I also don't want my new husband and or his family to feel slighted, or as if they have to compete for our time and loyalty. What can I do?

Loyal to All

### *Response*

Dear Loyal,

How fortunate you are to have two sets of loving and accepting in-laws! This is a rare thing, indeed. Most parents, no matter what their sons or daughters have done, feel loyal to their own children and find a way to reject their daughters-in-law or sons-in-law. (See next letter.) Because you do have such a good relationship with your in-laws, you should be able to keep them in your life. Keep in mind, though, that your new parents-in-law have priority for you and your new husband, while your children may still feel, at least for a while, that their original grandparents are most important. Because of these differences in emotional loyalty, you'll have to give the time you spend together with each set of in-laws a lot of advance planning and thought.

**Remember that love is not finite, and you can love as many people as you have room in your life to love.**

If you want to be with your former in-laws as a family, and if your new husband is comfortable with the idea, have them over for dinner regularly. If this is not comfortable for him, have lunch or coffee with your former mother-in-law when you can, and maintain your relationship with them apart from your new husband in ways that do not really leave him out, such as keeping in touch by phone and e-mail.

Be careful of holidays. Don't expect to be part of your former in-law's family celebrations any longer. This is one of the unfortunate losses people experience from divorce. During these special and emotionally fraught events, make your family and your new husband's family a priority, knowing that your kids will get to see their dad's parents during holiday time when they are with him.

You must be a very special person to inspire such love. Remember that love is not finite, and you can love as many people as you have room in your life to love.

> *Being confident of this, that he who began a good work in you will carry it on to completion until the day of Christ Jesus.*
>
> —*Philippians 1:6*

> *And this is my prayer: that your love may abound more and more in knowledge and depth of insight, so that*

> *you may be able to discern what is best and may be pure and blameless until the day of Christ.*
>
> *—Philippians 1:9–10*

God bless you!
Margaret

. . . . . . . . . . . . . . . . . . . . . . . . . . . . . . . . . . . .

## *Question*

Dear Margaret,

I've always liked my mother-in-law and consider her a dear friend. Through the years, she's often helped me garden and has always been involved in our lives. My ex-husband, her son, is an abuser. As he became more and more abusive, I hid it from her. She adores him, so I doubted that she would ever believe me if I told her about it.

When I filed for divorce she became enraged. She has not spoken to me since, except for one time when I tried to explain to her about the abuse. She literally made fun of me and made light of what happened, more than implying that it wasn't really abuse. I hate to lose her friendship, and I hate to have her think so ill of me when I did everything I could to stay in our marriage. (After I had a complete emotional breakdown, both my therapist and family doctor told me I needed to leave to be safe and healthy.)

Is there any way I can preserve my friendship with her? Is there any way to make her understand?

I am,
Feeling the Loss

## *Response*

Dear Feeling the Loss,

Yours is a sad but typical story. When people get divorced, parents are usually loyal to their own children, no matter how close they were to their children-in-law. Your ex-husband is, after all, their own son. They'll find any way they can to criticize you in order to justify what he's done, because if they don't the divorce would kill them. They have to believe that it was your fault because it's the only way they can bring themselves to accept it.

**We eventually learn how to weave the pain we've experienced into the fabric of our lives.**

No, you will not be able to still be friends with your mother-in-law. It's one of the losses of your divorce. You may grieve the loss of her friendship for a long time. Such grief is normal. Losses of every kind hurt, and we don't really "get over" many of those losses. Rather, we eventually learn how to weave the pain we've experienced into the fabric of our lives.

It's possible that your husband learned his patterns of abuse from his own parents, and his mother, in order to survive, has had to explain it away all her married life, refusing to call it the abuse it is. If this is true then of course she must deny your abuse as well.

May the God of all comfort and peace comfort you as you accept the many and varied losses of your divorce. Let the prayer of Jeremiah be yours:

> *Heal me, O LORD, and I will be healed; save me and I will be saved, for you are the one I praise.*
>
> —*Jeremiah 17:14*

And be assured, as Isaiah was, that,

> *He heals the brokenhearted and binds up their wounds.*
> *—Psalm 147:3*

Rejoice as you receive this promise:

> *But for you who revere my name, the sun of righteousness will rise with healing in its wings. And you will go out and leap like calves released from the stall.*
> *—Malachi 4:2*

May God heal you and rebuild your life,
Margaret

## Chapter 11

# Dealing with the Ex

### *Question*

Dear Margaret,

I'm so fed up with my husband's ex-wife that I could scream! She uses us as a free baby-sitting service, calling at the spur of the moment to drop their two kids off whenever she feels like it. They aren't bad kids, but we have two children of our own, and I work full time. It'd be nice to have her keep to the visitation schedule so that we can make plans, and so that I can have some time on the weekends without the extra kids.

When we say no, she leaves her children with friends or relatives who are less than reliable people and who are of questionable character. When my husband tries to talk to her about being more consistent with the schedule or taking better care of the children, she just shrugs it off.

He says he'd rather have his kids with us than with her family or those creepy friends of hers, but I'm growing resentful because of the workload. How can we get his ex-wife to be more responsible and stick to the visitation schedule?

Overloaded Stepmom

## *Response*

Dear Overloaded,

You cannot make your husband's ex-wife do anything. Her behavior, as you may well realize, is beyond your control. Her irresponsibility is probably one of the things that ended her first marriage. As you already know, because of her instability, your stepchildren need the stabilizing influence and security of your home all the more. Your options are not many. Because you can't change her, and the children aren't going to disappear, you need to conceive of ways to live with the situation.

Just as your husband says, he must be there for his kids. That means they come into your home frequently, *but he himself can do a lot to lighten your load.* When his children come, whether it's planned in advance or not, he needs to be the one who spends the bulk of the time with them. If he's interacting with all the kids, playing with them, monitoring their play and behavior, it can take a big load from your shoulders.

**Your stepchildren need to be treated as members of the family, not as guests and not as people that you wait upon.**

Your stepchildren need to be treated as members of the family, not as guests and not as people that you wait upon. Along with the other children, they should have chores, and each person in your home needs to be responsible for his or her possessions. In other words, you need to operate as if you have four children instead of two. If you consider your husband's children members of the family, and design your schedule and your home to be a family of six instead of a family of four, things should work out better.

As far as making plans, as much as you can, plan as if they'll be there. Then if they're not, you have fewer people but will be prepared.

If you have plans to go away alone together, and your husband's children are foisted upon you at the last minute, have a ready-made back-up plan. Here are some ideas: Do they miss their grandparents?

Would they like to go there sometimes? Or, do they love your extended family or share any of the same friends as your children? What about making friends at church with someone who has kids the same age and letting his kids spend time with them? Then this family too could become a back-up place for your stepchildren to stay when you have couple-time planned. These suggestions are of course only for the occasional special event—not to be made a habit. To sum it up: if you are making overnight plans for your own kids, make some for your husband's kids too, just in case they show up.

**When the behavior of your husband's ex is rude and disruptive, don't take it out on the children by making them feel unwanted.**

Please check your attitude. When the behavior of your husband's ex is rude and disruptive, don't take it out on the children by making them feel unwanted. It's hard to allow someone to take advantage of you as she is, but the children are the greater concern, and for their protection and well-being your home needs to be a place of welcome for them.

Living with your situation is not an easy thing, but when you married your husband, it came with the package. We're sorry that she's making the deal so difficult. May God give both you and your husband strength.

> *But he [Jesus] said to me, "My strength is sufficient for you, for my power is made perfect in weakness." Therefore I will boast all the more gladly about my weaknesses, so that Christ's power may rest on me. That is why, for Christ's sake, I delight in weaknesses, in insults, in hardships, in persecutions, in difficulties. For when I am weak, then I am strong.*
>
> —*2 Corinthians 12:9–10*

May He give you strength,
Margaret

## *Question*

Dear Margaret,

My husband and I both have shared custody of our biological children. I'm a stay-at-home-mom who is devoted to raising all of our children to the best of my abilities. The problem is my husband's ex-wife. Whenever we go to sporting events, school programs, and so forth, she gets verbally abusive toward me. She says things like, "What are you doing here? You have no right to be here! I'm their mother! You are not!" Now she's said that if I continue to show up at our children's events, she'll make our lives miserable.

The children want all of their parents to be present for their special events, and we both want to be supportive for all of our children. Help!

Embarrassed for Me and Sad for the Kids

## *Response*

Dear Embarrassed,

It's wonderful that you want to be there for both your children and your stepchildren, but it sounds like you need a time-out to allow the emotions to cool. So take time off. For a time or two, don't go to your stepchildren's school events. (Certainly don't hold back if your birthchildren are involved, however!) In this time, try to communicate with your husband's ex. If she won't talk to you, go through a third party—your husband, a teacher, or use a letter. In this communication, assure her that you clearly understand that she's the children's mother. *Assure the birthmother that you're not trying to take her place. Ask her what she'd like your role to be.* Ask her if there's any way that you can work out something like coming to events and sit-

***Assure the birthmother that you're not trying to take her place.***

ting on the opposite side of the room, or if she would be more comfortable with the two of you taking turns in coming. Through the intermediary tell her that because she's the birthmother, you're giving her these choices, but eventually you will be attending the children's events.

***The goal here is not for one of you to win or lose—the goal is to make both families winners.***

Right now she's filled with hostility and resentment because the family that was once hers, both husband and children, are now with you. Even if the divorce was her idea, she's hurting from the loss of her nuclear family. It may be hard for you to let her have a voice; you may feel like you're losing a battle. *But the goal here is not for one of you to win or lose—the goal is to make both families winners.*

Your stepchildren are her children, and her biological instincts are to protect and possess them. So right now she's acting on instinct and emotion rather than on intellect. Your goal, to resolve this, is to help her be more rational by trying to communicate in as noncombative a way as possible.

Something you may consider, for the long haul, if you can discuss things with her, is the possibility of dividing the parenting responsibilities. Since you have shared custody, one of you, for example, could be in charge of haircuts and clothes buying. The other could be the main homework helper and research assistant for papers and big projects. Focus on what you're best at. Since she's the one with the anger, diffuse her anger by asking her if there's part of her job of parenting that she hates doing. Maybe taking the children to the doctor, the dentist, or doing the leaf-gathering for the fifth grade leaf project are things she'd rather not do. Find out what she really doesn't want to do and volunteer to do that with the children. Later, volunteer to do the thing you love most. Perhaps it will be different from the things she loves. *We hope that gradually she'll view you as a parenting partner and not as a competitor.* But in order for this to happen, major communication must occur.

Be assured that many birthmoms and stepmoms have a degree of

**Many birthmoms and stepmoms have a degree of competitiveness when first entering this complicated blending family situation.**

competitiveness when first entering this complicated blending family situation. But give it time, keep attempting to communicate, be as nonthreatening as possible, take a time out and don't go to things for a bit, and gradually, together with her, begin to define your roles in your children's and stepchildren's lives.

More and more birthmoms and stepmoms are finding their way to this partnership, and everyone benefits when it can happen. Do an Internet search using the word "stepmom" and you'll get lots of good ideas on how to divide parenting jobs and time with her.

> *God has called us to live in peace.*
>
> *—1 Corinthians 7:15*

> *There are different kinds of gifts, but the same Spirit. There are different kinds of service, but the same Lord. There are different kinds of working, but the same God works all of them in all men.*
>
> *—1 Corinthians 12:4–6*

All the best as you work for growth and harmony!
Margaret

Chapter 12

# Blending Religions, Issues of Faith

## *Question*

Dear Margaret,

My fiancée and I are both Christians, but she's Catholic and I'm Baptist. We both go to our own churches with our children, and we both feel comfortable visiting each other's churches. I've tried to convince her that my religion is more biblical and, although she isn't able to defend her faith very well, she wants to stay Catholic.

We're hoping to get married in a nondenominational service, remain in our own faiths, each raising our own children in our respective faith. We don't plan to have any children together, but it's not impossible.

Our families are both horrified. My fiancée's mom says that if she gets married outside the church to a non-Catholic, her soul will be in danger of hell. My family says that it will be impossible to practice separate religions in one house. We point out that we already have Bible reading and prayers at dinner on the night of the week we're all together. Each weekend we decide which church to go to, and often we go our separate ways, but sometimes we go to one church or the other together. We don't see why this would have to change and why this couldn't work. What do you say?

Two Religions, One Faith

## *Response*

Dear Two Religions,

You are asking yourselves to do a very difficult thing. Perhaps answering the following questions will help you come to a decision:

1. Are both of you so tolerant that you'll have total respect for one another's religious beliefs all the time? That means no criticism or snide remarks or disrespect for traditions, and so forth. That means no "looks" or critical remarks when she practices her faith in your home.
2. Will you forever feel as if you have to work at changing your spouse? Please don't get married if you think you'll change the other person—it won't happen.
3. Will you be able to listen to your spouse teach his or her children about God and about the practices of his or her religion without feeling conflicted?
4. You said that having a child together was possible. What if you do? Can you agree on whether or not the child will be baptized in the Catholic faith? Who will get to take that child to church? You need to agree on the answer to this question now.
5. Will you be able to live with criticism from your parents and extended family? Consider the possibility that it may never end.
6. Could you live with the grandparents' telling your children that your marriage is wrong? (This happened constantly to some people we know.)
7. Depending on how strongly they feel, would you be able to live with total rejection by some or all of your extended family?

If you answer "no" to any one of these questions, it's likely that a great deal of pain will be brought into your blending.

We talked to a couple in this situation before they married. They promised to always be tolerant and respectful of each other's faith. But when they married, they found it impossible to do so. One spouse continually tries to persuade the other, and there is much criticism in the home—increased greatly by their having an unplanned child together. One spouse lives brokenhearted that the child is not baptized in the church, and the other lives in fear and dread that the child will be. Their lives have been unspeakably difficult. Their children have suffered a lot from this conflict, as they constantly hear their parents' marriage criticized by the grandparents. They have all suffered estrangement from various extended family members. It's a hard thing you're thinking of doing.

***Can two walk together, except they be agreed?***
***—Amos 3:3 (KJV)***

> *Can two walk together, except they be agreed?*
> *—Amos 3:3 (KJV)*

> *"Every kingdom divided against itself will be ruined, and every city or household divided against itself will not stand."*
> *—Matthew 12:25*

Please reconsider,
Margaret

## *Question*

Dear Margaret,

Both my fiancé and I became Christians after our divorces. Totally devastated, it was our newfound faith that saw us through those difficult times and brought us healing. All of that is behind us now. We met in our church's single-again ministry.

Since we're fairly new to the faith, we were wondering what the faith issues might be in blending our families. We each have school-aged children who come to church with us when we have them.

What questions should we be asking?

We Want to Get It Right This Time

## *Response*

Dear Want to Get it Right,

Congratulations on finding faith in Christ and in finding one another! We hope that your church or some organization near you has good premarital counseling. Please take advantage of it. Especially helpful is a premarriage test or questionnaire that can help you work through many of the issues of remarriage. If such counseling is not available to you, we recommend the workbooks for him and her, *Saving Your Second Marriage Before It Starts* by Leslie Parrott, and a book called *Willing to Try Again* by Dick Dunn.[1]

The following are questions to ask about your faith before remarriage. *Do not marry unless you have come to a consensus on the answers to these questions.*

1. How strongly do you feel about practicing your faith? Is one of you far more committed and far more involved than the other? This could be a potential area of conflict. Please discuss it.
2. Have you agreed upon a church where your whole family will attend? Saving this decision for after the marriage creates more stress while at the same time taking away one of the primary supports that will help you as you blend your new family.
3. How does being committed to following Christ play out in your lives? Will you both want to join a Bible study or other small group? If not, how will you each feel if one goes alone?

**Begin to pray together.**

4. Are you both committed to family time spent in Bible reading and prayer? If you are, decide upon a specific time when you'll do this. Will it be at the table? At bedtime? If you don't decide a time and place, it won't happen. If you decide to have devotions at the table, start them now whenever you have dinner at home together.
5. Are you both committed to keeping God's commandments and to teaching them to your children?
6. If you haven't already, begin to pray together. Not only will it be good practice for your marriage, you'll be amazed at the growth in your intimacy when you share in this way.

We're glad you're asking questions now. Please do get a workbook to do together or go to a premarital class or workshop.

We're so glad that through your trials you've found faith in Christ our Savior.

> *Trust in the* Lord *with all your heart and lean not on your own understanding; in all your ways acknowledge him, and he will make your paths straight.*
>
> —*Proverbs 3:5–6*

> *For God so loved the world that he gave his one and only Son, that whoever believes in him shall not perish but have eternal life.*
>
> —*John 3:16*

May the Lord bless your blended Christian home,
Margaret

Chapter 13

# Etiquette for Blended Families

## *Question*

Dear Margaret,

My fiancé and I will be married soon. Each of us has been married before, and we both have children. Our children are in upper-elementary school, and I know they'll want to remain attached not only to their birthparents, but to their extended birthfamily as well. I'm thinking that things like graduation open-houses, funerals, and weddings could become very confusing and uncomfortable. When should we attend, when should we not? Do we sit with family? When we host a life-event type party, who do we invite? And so forth. Are there any guidelines for etiquette in the stepfamily?

We Just Want to Get It Right

## *Response*

Dear Right,

I'm so glad that you are trying to discover ahead of time the kindest and most thoughtful behavior in the emotionally sensitive situations of remarriage. The first thing to remember about etiquette is that it exists for the purpose of treating one another well. Good manners are not a list of meaningless social rules one must follow; they are guidelines for kindness and consideration of others.

**Etiquette . . . exists for the purpose of treating one another well.**

When we eat, for example, napkins go into the lap, because dirty napkins are not nice for others to look at. We say "please" and "thank you" because doing so recognizes the value of the person of whom we are making a request and acknowledges that you're asking that person to inconvenience himself or herself for you.

In considering etiquette for the funerals, weddings, and graduations of your former extended family, ask yourself what would be kindest for all involved. In most cases, if you do what you and your current spouse and kids are comfortable with, it will be the right thing.

Most of the time, your children will attend the functions of your former extended family with their other birthparent. But if their other birthparent is deceased and the children are still young, you may be pressed into service to accompany them.

**For events that you're hosting for your children, invite everyone that is important in their lives—everyone they love!**

For events that you're hosting for your children, invite everyone that is important in their lives—everyone they love!

### *Funerals and Weddings*

In the case of funerals, the death of a former extended-family member is like that of anyone else you may know. If you knew the deceased and wish to honor him or her, then by all means you go to the funeral. You don't expect to be treated as a member of the family, but you go as a friend and as one who grieves.

Any function at which your current spouse and/or children need you to be with them, you will go. Your current spouse will come, in turn, to functions of your former extended family, to support you if you need him or her. You may attend alone if you are comfortable, as may your spouse.

If your children are included in the family seating at the wedding or funeral of a former extended-family member, you decide—are they old enough and mature enough to sit through a funeral or wedding if you're not beside them? If not, they sit with you in the non-family rows. If, on the other hand, the family of the deceased or family of the bride/groom invites you to sit in the family rows, it would be insensitive not to.

**Invite everyone you or your children love. It's up to the invitees whether or not they choose to come.**

What is the "proper" seating at weddings and the "proper posing" for wedding pictures when the bride/groom has stepparents as well as living birthparents? Judith Martin—author of the humorous national bestseller *Miss Manners' Guide to Excruciatingly Correct Behavior*—has some great comments,

> What do you mean by "proper etiquette"? Do you imagine that there exists somewhere, a stone diagram indicating the correct placement of sequential spouses according to some staid tradition? How many people do you figure that such a chart will allow in each collection of parents or grandparents?[1]

Martin says that the newlywed couple will use a sensible and gracious way to arrange people. They pose for their pictures with one set of parents and then the other. You do not force ex-spouses together, and you don't leave anyone out. In short—do the kindest thing. If you aren't sure what the kindest thing is for the people involved, ask them!

**Be there for your children no matter what.**

It's unfair for any stepparent or former extended-family member to say such awful things as, "If you invite him/her I won't come." Don't listen to such nonsense! It's time to put the past behind. If you're doing the inviting, you invite everyone you or your children love. It's up to the invitees whether or not they choose to come.

### *Graduation Open-Houses*

When our two oldest children graduated at the same time, we foolishly had four different open-houses! Some were just dinners, but still, how stupid was that for the finances and stress level? We learned our lesson. For the rest of the three children, we had one big bash, and it was great.

So from our own experience, I recommend that when you throw a graduation open-house for your children and stepchildren, include absolutely everyone! This event is to honor the kid and is not about you and any bad feelings you may have toward your former spouse and his or her family. Talk to your kids' birthparents. Find out who wants to throw the party and be there for your children no matter what. Be pleasant, be kind (even when others are not)—you will live! Seriously, you will live to see your children rise up and call you blessed!

One stepmom I know has thrown graduation open-houses for all of her biological children as well as custodial stepchildren. Yes, of course, it was stressful, but not unbearably so. She had the help and support of a wonderful husband, great sisters, and all the other kids. The children were ecstatically happy to have all their parents and all the people they love together to honor them. For their sakes, it was worth it.

### *Cards and Flowers*

Sending of cards is a great way to bridge the gap in dicey relationships. Suppose your children have a "wicked stepmother" or stepfather that kicks them out of the house. That stepparent should still get cards from them on special occasions, such as Mother's Day or Father's Day. Rebuilding your children's broken relationship with that stepparent is essential to their being able to stay in their birthparent's life. Someone has to begin the healing. Why not let it be you? There are great cards on the market that have neutral but respectful messages for every occasion from Mother's Day to Christmas to "just because."

If you're a Christian, do as Jesus said, "Love one another." And, "Do to others what you would have them do to you" (Matt. 7:12). He didn't say, "Do as you have been done to"! Always do the kinder thing. The sending of cards, flowers, or other small and mailable gifts for special occasions is, in fact, a wonderful way to tell a person that he or she is important in your life, even if your relationship is not all that harmonious at the moment. No matter how strained you may feel in someone's presence, if that person has been instrumental in your upbringing or is married to one of your parents or children, with these small tokens on appropriate holidays you can acknowledge that person's value in your life and his or her value as a person who God created.

I'm really into e-mail cards. The nominal annual fee is well worth my being able to send a greeting in a minute without going shopping.

For more tips, check out Miss Manners. You can find her book at most public libraries. Look under *stepparents* in the index in the back of her book, and you'll find a wonderful guide to many uncomfortable stepfamily situations. Her humor helps put such things in the proper perspective.

Remember, in all of these things, to do as Jesus said:

> *My command is this: "Love each other as I have loved you."*
>
> —*John 15:12*

Another guideline given by the Lord Himself is found in Luke 6:27–28:

> *"But I tell you who hear me: Love your enemies, do good to those who hate you, bless those who curse you, pray for those who mistreat you."*

May God give you wisdom as you strive to do the loving thing,
Margaret

Chapter 14

# Blending Finances and Legal Matters

I'm not a legal or financial expert—only a stepparent who has learned a lot along the way. *My advice is not a substitute for professional guidance in these areas.*

## *Question*

Dear Margaret,

My fiancée and I are engaged to be married in a few months and will be blending two kids each. Could you please give us some idea of the things we need to think about when it comes to finances and other legal matters? We're nervous about doing something that will end up being detrimental down the road.

Thanks a lot!

We are,
Cautious and a Bit Apprehensive

## *Response*

Dear Cautious and Apprehensive,

I applaud you on wanting to be prepared and have all your bases covered. Many people enter into remarriage far too quickly without enough regard to these matters.

***You risk doing great harm to your marriage if you allow unresolved conflict over financial matters to persist.***

Other than problems with the children, conflict over money is the most commonly cited reason for a second divorce. It is crucial, therefore, that a couple has good communication in this area.

Below are general areas of consideration, questions to ask, and decisions to make about finances before you remarry. For those reading this book who are already married, review what you find below and make sure that you've done everything you can to blend finances. *Do not hesitate to consult a marriage counselor or a financial planner if you have any areas upon which you cannot agree. You risk doing great harm to your marriage if you allow unresolved conflict over financial matters to persist.*

### *To Blend or Not to Blend: Where Will the Money Go?*

You will have to decide if you want joint or separate checking and savings accounts. If child support is coming in, some couples may choose to keep separate accounts. Other couples pool all of their money.

If you decide to combine all funds, be sure that you can account for, in writing, how all the child support money is spent. The person paying the support has a right to this information, and you don't want to be caught being unaccountable. The house payment and cost of utilities, for example, can be divided by the number of people in your home to find the individual child's share of what it costs for him or her to live there. Keep track of the cost of clothing, dental and medical bills, and so forth.

**Having a current will is always important, but in a blended family, it's crucial.**

If you decide to keep funds separate, how much knowledge of those funds will you share with your spouse? We recommend complete disclosure. If you don't intend to be completely forthcoming about the money you receive from your ex, your fiancé or spouse needs to know why you have taken this position.

*Who Owns What?*

Whose name/names will be on the title to your home? Your cars? Your investments? If you owned such large ticket items before remarriage, will you now own them jointly, or will you maintain separate ownership?

*Who Gets What?*

Unless you state otherwise in a legal will, when you die, all of your assets will go to your current spouse.

If you want a part of your assets held in trust for your children, you need to consult a lawyer about setting up a will and trust. Do not delay in doing this! We have friends who, after only two years of marriage, are facing his coming death by cancer. Young children are involved.

We have another friend whose father just died. Because the father did not have a will, his entire large estate went to his wife of only two years. His children received nothing. Having a current will is always important, but in a blended family, it's crucial.

*Retirement, Social Security Payments, and So Forth*

If you were married twenty years or more to your former spouse, he or she may be entitled to half of your retirement account and some, if not all, of your social security benefits when you die. Make sure you know whether or not your ex is still entitled to your retirement assets. Often, if you have had thorough lawyers and a good judge at your divorce, this has already been settled. Ask yourself if it has. Get legal advice if it has not.

**Discuss priorities and settle on what is important before your differences about spending become an issue.**

### *Budgets*

Set up a monthly budget together, and plan how you will spend your money. Discuss priorities and settle on what is important before your differences about spending become an issue.

### *Children and Money*

Will your children get an allowance? Will they have to do chores to receive it? We strongly suggest that the same standards and awards apply to all children living in the house and to those who may come for visitation. Come to an agreement about this behind closed doors so that, to the children, you present a united front.

Will you help fund the children's college education? Where will the money come from? How will you make it grow? Will all the children receive an equal share? Will they have separate college money based upon what you brought into the marriage? How does the contribution of the other birthparent factor in toward higher education?

### *To Give or Not to Give—That Can Be a Question*

How much of your income do you believe should be given to your church or other charities? Discuss this and come to an agreement about it. God will bless you if you give.

He says,

> *Remember this: Whoever sows sparingly will also reap sparingly, and whoever sows generously will also reap generously. Each man should give what he has decided in his heart to give, not reluctantly or under compulsion, for God loves a cheerful giver. And God is able to make all grace abound to you, so that in all things at*

> *all times, having all that you need, you will abound in every good work.*
>
> *—2 Corinthians 9:6–8*

May God give you wisdom,
Margaret

. . . . . . . . . . . . . . . . . . . . . . . . . . . . . . . . . . . . .

## *Question*

Dear Margaret,

My first husband was a plastic surgeon with a successful practice and an unbelievable income. He was also so driven he never had time for our marriage. As I became more demanding, he became abusive and unfaithful.

Now I'm married to a kind and loving man. We spend all of our time together when we're not at work. Although we're financially comfortable, our combined income is considerably less than what my first husband made . . . and I couldn't care less. We've been married two years, and I love the life we share . . . except that my husband cannot forget how I used to live. Periodically he gets depressed that we can't go on expensive vacations or buy designer clothing. I enjoy our simple, easy-to-clean home, but at least once a year he goes into a funk about it being inferior to what I had before.

How can I convince my husband that I'm happy with him and with our lifestyle? How can I get him to stop feeling like he's in competition with my first husband? There's simply no competition!

Happy and I Know It!

## *Response*

Dear Happy,

I'm glad that you're happy with your new life. I'd like you to do a little self-examination. If you can answer no to all the questions, then the problem is not yours, but your husband's. You cannot control how he feels. You can only reassure him as needed.

Here's the test. Do you ever talk about your past home in a wistful way? Do you mention with longing the stores in which you used to shop? Do you charge more than you can afford to pay each month, thereby making your husband feel financially pressured? If you're doing any of these, it may be contributing to your husband's feelings and you need to stop doing them. If you're doing none of them, then his feelings are really his problem. There's only so much you can do about how he feels.

***"Forget the former things; do not dwell on the past. See, I am doing a new thing! Now it springs up; do you not perceive it?"***
***—Isaiah 43:18–19***

It is possible that your husband needs his self-esteem built up in general. There are several Christian books on the market that deal with this topic. Two popular titles are *What Makes a Man Feel Loved* by Bob Burnes, and *Building Your Mate's Self-Esteem* by Dennis and Barbara Rainey.

Your husband may be prone to depression, or it's possible that something else about your marriage is bothering him and this is the way he expresses it. We recommend that the two of you explore these possibilities with the help of a marriage counselor.

Encourage your husband from the Scripture as well:

> *"Forget the former things;*
> *do not dwell on the past.*

*See, I am doing a new thing!*
*Now it springs up; do you not perceive it?"*
*—Isaiah 43:18–19*

God bless your new life,
Margaret

## *Question*

Dear Margaret,

My heart is breaking! My husband pays so much child support that we can't afford to have a child of our own. If we have a baby (I've never had children), I want to stay home and raise it, but I wouldn't be able to stop working because my income pays most of our bills, while most of his income goes to his ex.

**Although natural parents are legally and financially obligated to support their children until the kids reach eighteen, the actual amount of child support payments are not set in stone.**

When I married my husband, I already knew and loved his two children; we got along very well. It was, in fact, in the enjoyment that I received from his children that I realized this was the man with whom I wanted to have a child—this was the man I would marry. He has a good job, so I never dreamed that finances would be so tight. He wants to have a baby, too, and my biological clock is ticking away, but we're afraid we simply can't afford it. Is there anything we can do?

Strapped and Breaking

## *Response*

Dear Strapped,

Don't break! There's hope. First, although natural parents are legally and financially obligated to support their children until the kids reach eighteen, the actual amount of child support payments are not set in stone. They can be subject to change when your husband's income and/or responsibilities change. Your having a child may be a factor in making such an adjustment. Policies vary from state to state; that's why it's important to have a lawyer to act as your advocate. It's unfortunate that lawyers, too, cost money, but you'll need legal expertise. Choose a lawyer who specializes in helping parents with custody and support issues. Perhaps the state in which you live will acknowledge the need for part of his income to support any child he'll have, not just the ones from his previous marriage.

Your husband may be able to petition the Friend of the Court for more parenting time. If he's able to obtain joint or shared custody, which equals a certain number of hours per week, then his child support would be reduced or perhaps eliminated entirely. More and more couples are opting for shared custody, and, as far as we can see, everybody is a winner. The kids get to spend more time with their birthparents, and the parents get a financial break. Shared custody also reaps the happy result of avoiding the "Disneyland Dad" syndrome. If children spend equal or nearly equal amounts of time in each home, they'll be less likely to feel like a guest and more likely to feel as if they have two real homes. Shared custody is not usually every other day back and forth, as it may sound, although it could mean that. Often it consists of lengthening the weekends one parent already has the kids and having the children overnight one day every week.

**If children spend equal or nearly equal amounts of time in each home, they'll be less likely to feel like a guest and more likely to feel as if they have two real homes.**

If you come to this kind of legal agreement, maintain good communication with your husband's ex-wife. Decide whose insurance covers the kids, who'll take them to the doctor, who'll drive them where, and so forth. *Make an attempt to equally divide not only the time but the responsibility for the children.*

Don't give up hope of having a child together. Get legal help. As much as it costs, it'll be worth it in the long run.

Examine your heart. Make sure that you and your husband both are making the well-being of your family, and of his children, your first priority. God says,

> *Whoever can be trusted with very little can also be trusted with much, and whoever is dishonest with very little will also be dishonest with much. So if you have not been trustworthy in handling worldly wealth, who will trust you with true riches?*
>
> —*Luke 16:10–11*

Our children are our true riches!

> *"Seek ye first the kingdom of God, and his righteousness; and all these things will be added unto you."*
>
> —*Matt. 6:33* KJV

May you have hope and see grace,
Margaret

## *Question*

Dear Margaret,

Since my divorce, my ex-husband has paid child support for the children and, consequently, he had the right to the full exemption for them on his income tax. He wants us to change the custody agreement to shared custody and 50/50 on child support. I'm feeling agreeable to his suggestion but if we do this, who gets to claim the children as exemptions? Before I agree to this arrangement, could you please comment?

Cautious

## *Response*

Dear Cautious,

This is an area that is greatly facilitated by having a good relationship with your children's father. According to page 262 of *The Complete Idiot's Guide to Stepparenting* by Ericka Lutz, "Child support is tax free to the receiver and it is not a deductible expense for the payee. . . . Legally, the person who has custody the most is eligible for the deduction [i.e., exemption]."[2] This has been your experience so far. But if you agree to a shared custody agreement, "Only one household can claim a child as a tax exemption each year."[3] You don't mention how many children you have, but if it's an even number, you could each claim half the children (although not half a child). If you have two children, for example, each of you could claim one of them. If you have four, each could claim two, and so forth. We have friends who do this; he claims the boy, she claims the girl. Or you could take turns each year, first one of you takes the exemption, and the following year, the other biological parent takes the exemption.

If a non-custodial parent claims a child as an exemption, a special tax form must be filed, and the signature of the other parent is then required.

Please keep in mind that tax laws change frequently, and it always pays to consult a professional tax preparer.

> *Jesus . . . said, . . . "Show me the coin used for paying the tax." They brought him a denarius, and he asked them, "Whose portrait is this? And whose inscription?"*

> *"Caesar's," they replied. Then he said to them, "Give to Caesar what is Caesar's, and to God what is God's."*
>
> *—Matthew 22:18–21*

All the best,
Margaret

## *Question*

Dear Margaret,

When Alan and I met, we knew exactly how much the other made because we work for the same company. His position is secure (at least as much as it can be in this day and age) and his income generous. I never dreamed that in marrying him I'd be on the brink of financial disaster! He's so far in debt that my good credit standing is threatened, and we can't even make ends meet!

I feel angry and betrayed. When we talked about money before our marriage, I learned how much he paid for child support payments and the amount of his house payment. Now I find out that he has a second mortgage and many thousands of dollars in credit card debt. I don't think I'm a scrooge, but I've never charged more than I could pay each month. I have money in savings, as well as a small investment. Now my clean record and savings are at risk because he can't cover all his monthly payments.

He is ever an optimist and doesn't get as upset about his debt as I do, and he can't see why I feel angry with him. I'd have never married him had I known all this, or at the very least I'd have waited until he got some of his debts paid. But I did marry him, and now I don't know what to do. I want our marriage to last, but I'm scared because I feel like running.

Do you have any advice?

Threatened

## *Response*

Dear Threatened,

First of all, run as fast as you can—but not away from your husband! *Run, with your husband to a good financial advisor, preferably one who understands the dynamics of second marriages.* The good news is, the scenario you outlined is a common one and you'll be able to find help. The bad news is, you're correct when you assume that all he has is yours, and all you have is his . . . including the debt. It's possible that divorcing him would not free you from his financial burden. An experienced professional financial adviser will help you to find several creative solutions for dealing with his debt.

**You're correct when you assume that all he has is yours, and all you have is his . . . including the debt.**

You both would also benefit from marriage counseling to help you deal with your resentment and to help him understand your fear.

Your husband, too, must *stop spending now.* If he has not already done so, I recommend that he cut up his credit cards. You'll have to prioritize the debt you now share, and slowly tackle it. You mention the mortgages. Perhaps he'll need to sell the house and scale down to something with a lower house payment in order to save your investments yet still get out of debt.

He may have to take a temporary second job in order to pay off his credit cards. For the sake of your marriage, he should be the one to work the hardest to pay off his debt. The marriage counselor may be able to help convince him of this if he doesn't already agree.

**The best thing for couples thinking of remarriage is, of course, complete financial disclosure.**

The best thing for couples thinking of remarriage is, of course, complete financial disclosure. I'm sorry that you didn't have it. I hope that, with help, the two of you can find a way out from under this burden.

I'm pleased to hear from your letter that you've been faithful with the income God has given to you. Perhaps you can be encouraged and encourage your husband with this verse, challenging him to obey it: "Now it is required that those who have been given a trust must prove faithful" (1 Cor. 4:2). Because you've been faithful, God will bless you: "A faithful man [or woman] will be richly blessed" (Prov. 28:20).

If you both go to God for help, seeking wisdom, God promises to give it:

> *If any of you lacks wisdom, he [she] should ask God, who gives generously to all without finding fault, and it will be given to him [her].*
>
> —*James 1:5*

Help your husband get out of debt, and hear this blessing from the Lord:

> *"Well done, good and faithful servant! You have been faithful with a few things; I will put you in charge of many things. Come and share your master's happiness!"*
>
> —*Matthew 25:21*

Get the help and support that you need right away, and may God bless your faithfulness as you both climb out of this debt.

All the best in the kingdom,
Margaret

## *Question*

Dear Margaret,

My ex-husband almost never makes his child support payments. If he does, they don't come on time. What can I do about this?

It's not just me, but my kids that are getting the raw deal. We really need that money!

I Feel Shafted

## *Response*

Dear Shafted,

You're not helpless in this matter. Each state may have its own method of doing things, and different names for the departments to which you should go for legal help. Every state, however, has recourse for enforcing child support rulings.

If you know how, report your ex-husband to the Friend of the Court, a representative from the family and domestic court. Keep a written record of exactly when he pays, how much he pays, and the dates when he doesn't pay. Keep a copy for yourself and turn one over to the court representative with whom you have contact. If the court finds him in violation, they'll refer the case to law enforcement, and a warrant can be issued for his arrest for nonpayment of child support.

**If anyone does not provide for his relatives, and especially for his immediate family, he has denied the faith and is worse than an unbeliever.**
**—1 Timothy 5:8**

According to *Stepping Stones for Stepfamilies,* "The Child Support Enforcement program can help locate an absent parent, identify the amount of the support obligation, and enforce the support order."[4] Look in your local telephone directory under the name of the state in which you live and try key words like *family court, friend of the court, child support enforcement,* and so forth. If you can't figure out who to call by looking there, simply call the police and ask them who you should call.

You have every right to do this. The Bible says, "If anyone does not provide for his relatives, and especially for his immediate family, he has denied the faith and is worse than an unbeliever" (1 Tim. 5:8).

I hope that very soon your children's father will do his share in supporting them, and in the meantime, we pray that God will provide your every need.

> *And my God will meet all your needs according to his glorious riches in Christ Jesus.*
>
> —*Philippians 4:19*

May the Lord give you hope and strength,
Margaret

## *Question*

Dear Margaret,

My stepchildren are thirteen, eleven, and eight years old. I love them like my own. My husband and I have been married for six years, and I've been a partner with my husband in raising his children every step of the way. Sometimes they've lived with us full time, sometimes they haven't. Right now the thirteen year old is back with her mom, but comes often enough that the courts consider us to have shared custody. The other two are with us most of the time right now, along with my two children. The children all feel like brothers and sisters; for the most part we feel like one family. Long ago their mother and I learned how to work together for the good of the kids.

**Legally speaking, you have no rights to your stepchildren after your husband's death.**

Now my husband, the father of these beautiful children, is dying of cancer. His will is in order, and I'm satisfied with the financial arrangements he's made, both for us and for his children.

But my problem, Margaret, concerns

his children. What rights will I have to my stepchildren after he dies? I feel like it will kill me not only to lose him, but to lose the children, too! It would be a terrible thing to go to court over something like this right now. I haven't even had the courage to bring up this subject with the children's mother. Could you just tell me please what my rights are?

Already Grieving

## *Response*

Dear Grieving,

We applaud you for the adjustments that you've made and the success you've made of stepparenting. How sad for you now! We're sorry to hear of your husband's illness—and it does get sadder. Legally speaking, you have no rights to your stepchildren after your husband's death. Since you and his ex-wife right now have an open and good relationship, we suggest that you go to her and ask if she'd be willing to make a visitation agreement with you for the time after your husband dies. Set the agreement down in writing.

Requests of this kind have been taken to court and the petitioner received some visitation rights. This is unusual and, of course, the petitioners had to have legal counsel. We recommend that you at least consult with an attorney who's familiar with the law and, most importantly, the precedent of your state. Please do so immediately.

If you are as bonded with these children as you say, they'll want to be with you, and perhaps their mother will listen to their requests to see you.

During the death of our respective spouses, my husband and I were each aware of the presence of God. We could sometimes tangibly feel ourselves being held up by the prayers of God's people. We will pray the same will be your experience—that this will be, in fact, your experience now.

> *Praise be to the God and Father of our Lord Jesus Christ, the Father of compassion and the God of all comfort, who comforts us in all our troubles, so that we can comfort those in any trouble with the comfort we ourselves have received from God. For just as the sufferings of Christ flow over into our lives, so also through Christ our comfort overflows.*
>
> *—2 Corinthians 1:3–5*

May God bless you and may His spirit fill you with comfort and a strong awareness of His presence during this difficult time.

Margaret

## *Question*

Dear Margaret,

I will soon marry a woman with children, and I want to be a good stepfather. Their dad is involved in their lives and pays child support. What I want to know is, just what are my legal rights and responsibilities to my stepchildren? For how much of their support am I responsible? What are reasonable obligations?

**Your stepparenting obligations are mostly emotional and spiritual.**

Want to Do It Right

## *Response*

Dear Right,

We applaud your responsible intentions and your good heart! We hope that you will partner with your new spouse in raising her children, but your stepparenting obligations are mostly emotional and spiritual. You'll be in a position to be of great influence. If the children are young enough, you may actually parent them. Using a book or other material that is age appropriate, you may lead your family in a time of spiritual devotion to God every night with Bible reading and prayer. We did this around the dinner table each night. It became a wonderful time of sharing, and an opportunity for much of our blending to take place. Please understand that your interaction with your stepchildren, especially when it comes to discipline, needs to evolve gradually. (See the chapter on "Blending Discipline.")

According to *Stepping Stones for Stepfamilies*, "As a general rule, stepparents have no obligation to support stepchildren." You need to know that "having stepchildren living in your home does not mean that you have the legal right for care and custody of them."[5] In a medical emergency, for example, you won't have the right to authorize treatment unless both birthparents have signed a consent form for you to do so. *Stepping Stones* warns that "this type of informal permission generally is not enough where substantial liability may exist."[6] We take this to mean that the decisions about surgery and such things as long-term medical treatment are up to the child's birthparents. You would, of course, support your wife and give her any wisdom you may have. But you probably wouldn't have decision-making rights.

**A well-blended family has two adults that are complete partners with equal power within the home.**

This is the bane of stepparenting. You may invest much emotional work and daily toil into raising the children. You may be a friend, a mentor, and even a parent-in-residence—all of which benefit the children. *A well-blended family has two adults that are complete partners with equal power within the home.* But you have no legal rights or responsibilities. Your obligations are, in essence, moral rather than legal.

If there were no other father in your stepchildren's lives, they might qualify to be covered by your insurance. But since they have a dad who supports them, your insurance probably won't cover them. Check with your insurance company.

Again, we applaud you for being an honorable man who wants to do the right thing. On many days, being a stepdad will seem like a burden and a challenge beyond what you are able to handle. But God's Word has a message for you in these times:

> *"You are the light of the world. A city on a hill cannot be hidden. Neither do people light a lamp and put it under a bowl. Instead they put it on its stand, and it gives light to everyone in the house. In the same way, let your light shine before [your stepchildren], that they may see your good deeds and praise your Father in heaven."*
>
> *—Matthew 5:14–16*

> *Do everything without complaining or arguing, so that you may become blameless and pure, children of God without fault in a crooked and depraved generation, in which you shine like stars in the universe as you hold out the word of life [to your stepchildren].*
>
> *—Philippians 2:14–16*

And one final promise:

> *The Lord will guide you always; he will satisfy your needs in a sun-scorched land and will strengthen your frame.*
>
> *—Isaiah 58:11*

May God richly bless your stepparenting,
Margaret

## *Question*

Dear Margaret,

I will soon marry a woman with two children. I have none of my own, but we hope to have one together. My fiancée's ex-husband deserted the family several years ago and hasn't been heard from since. She's never received a single child support payment or any kind of help from him. It's our intention that I will adopt her children.

My question is this: After I adopt them, can their birthfather come back and interfere in our lives? Will their names legally and permanently be the same as mine? Will I have full rights and obligations?

A Future Adoptive Dad

## *Response*

Dear Dad,

Before you'll be able to adopt your fiancée's children, a given number of years must pass in which the birthfather has been completely unheard from and uninvolved. Consult a lawyer about the necessary period.

**Don't be hurt or disappointed if, at some time in the future, your adopted children want to seek out their birthfather.**

As for your rights and responsibilities, we once again refer to *Stepping Stones for Stepfamilies* as our authoritative source. It says, "When stepchildren are adopted, legal rights and responsibilities between the children and their non-custodial natural parent no longer exist. An adopted child becomes the child of the adopting parent, just as if born to that parent."[7]

From a legal perspective, adoptive children are exactly the same as birthchildren. But don't be hurt or disappointed if, at some time in the future, your adopted children want to seek out their birthfather. As you may know, some people have a need to connect with their biological roots. If this does happen it won't necessarily be a reflection upon your parenting skills.

May God bless you, and may you become a real dad to those precious children, after God's own example in Romans 8:15–16:

> *For you did not receive a spirit that makes you a slave again to fear, but you received the Spirit of sonship. And by him we cry, "Abba [daddy], Father." The Spirit himself testifies with our spirit that we are God's children.*
>
> *For he chose us in him before the creation of the world to be holy and blameless in his sight. In love he predestined us to be adopted as his sons through Jesus Christ, in accordance with his pleasure and will.*
>
> —*Ephesians 1:4–5*

God bless you, Dad,
Margaret

## *Question*

Dear Margaret,

Both my fiancée and I were widowed young with school-aged children. We'll be married soon, and wonder what our legal rights and responsibilities are to the other's children.

We want our families to blend well and wonder if adopting each other's children would help. We also wonder if we need to adopt one another's children in order to legally make decisions in case of medical emergencies. We want to be real parents to one another's kids.

Good Dad

## *Response*

Dear Dad,

Roger and I are also both widowed. On the day that we married, I and my sons were automatically covered by my husband's health insurance plan. (We, of course, discussed this in advance with the insurance department of my husband's company.) Because we were both widowed, we automatically became legal guardians of one another's children. Because my children were under their stepdad's insurance plan, when my son got hit by a car, and his new dad was the first parent to arrive at the hospital, he was able to sign any and all permission needed. It's amazing how easy it is when you hold the insurance card that covers the child even when your last names are not the same.

**Because we were both widowed, we automatically became legal guardians of one another's children.**

A problem arises in emergencies only in a situation to which the biological parent could object. In our case, there was no other biological parent, and I certainly did not object to Roger being a fully responsible father to my sons. He, in turn, has always allowed me to take care of doctors' appointments for all of the children, including my stepdaughters. In the doctor's office, I'm the one who hands over the insurance card and signs on the bottom line. We both have had full medical authority for the children since the day of our marriage.

About adoption—we consulted a lawyer. She informed us that only one thing would change if we adopted one another's children—the social security benefits would stop. Because there is no other birthparent to contest the decisions we make, the lawyer said that there was no reason to go through the adoption process. Also, the boys didn't want to change their last name, and adopted children have the legal name of their adoptive parents. If you're concerned about everyone in your family having the same name, and the children are willing, you can make a legal name change without an adoption.

***What makes you a family is not your name. It's the memories you build and the lives that you share.***

We know a couple who, after widowhood and remarriage, adopted one another's children, yet the children never accepted their stepmother. After twenty years the stepmother still feels rejected, and the stepdaughters feel hateful and spiteful toward her. Her sons are like mere acquaintances to their stepfather. In contrast, our family never bothered with adoption, and we really have a blended family. Even though the boys' last name is Smith, the girls consider them their brothers, and they call the girls their sisters. We're the mom and the dad, the grandma and the grandpa, and there's no use of the word *step* among us.

*What makes you a family is not your name. It's the memories you build and the lives that you share.* We believe that the biggest "right and responsibility" of stepparents is to love their stepkids with all of their hearts, choosing love and kindness even when it doesn't feel natural, and having the courage to be the mom and the dad of the house even when the children object.

None of this happens overnight! At the end of four years, we thought we felt like a family; after seven years we felt even more blended; the day our first grandchild was born we knew we'd all become one. Blending is a process. But note—we are a blended family, not a nuclear family, and that's what we'll always be. For us, it's a wonderful thing, and we hope that your family will blend well.

I would like to share our wedding text with you:

*He has sent me to bind up the brokenhearted, . . .*
*to comfort all who mourn,*
*and provide for those who grieve in Zion—*
*to bestow on them a crown of beauty*
*instead of ashes,*
*the oil of gladness*
*instead of mourning,*
*and a garment of praise*

*instead of a spirit of despair.*
*They will be called oaks of righteousness,*
*a planting of the Lord*
*for the display of his splendor.*

*—Isaiah 61:1–3*

May God bless your blending, and may all of you become oaks of righteousness for the display of His splendor,
Margaret

## Chapter 15

# The Stepkids Speak

"Boy! If I had a chance to write a letter to my stepmom, I know what I'd say!" Several of the students in my college writing class expressed similar remarks when they learned I was writing this book. So I've included here a chapter from the perspective of stepkids.

I didn't stop with the letter of this college freshman and his classmates. Several years ago, I interviewed stepchildren from ages six to fifty-six, and a few of those responses are included as well. Some of these letters are addressed to me, some to the stepparent. Their experiences of living in a blended family should serve as an eye-opener to all of us.

***The strength and health of the marriage is vital to the security and happiness of the children.***

From almost all of these letters, you'll infer that *the strength and health of the marriage is vital to the security and happiness of the children.*

Their words have been edited for clarity, brevity, and anonymity.

Dear Stepmom,

Even though I was already a teenager when you married my dad, I'm glad that the two of you got together. It was sometimes difficult for me to adjust to your different ways of doing things. Sometimes I thought you were taking my dad away from me. But from this distance of years I can see that you're a good woman. My dad needed your love. You were a good wife to him and a good friend to me. Thank you for sharing in my life.

Connie (age fifty-six)

Dear Margaret,

I know that my stepmom loves me. She's a good wife to my dad. Even though she wasn't as affectionate as the mother I lost, she took an interest in my life, cheered me on, and saw that my needs were met. I think that we kids grew up pretty well, and I know that she had a lot to do with it.

Jodi (age thirty-six)

Dear Margaret,

I hate my stepmom, and I don't think she likes me very well either. I hate her because she always fights with my dad. I wish they'd stop fighting.

Rochelle (age ten)

Dear Stepmom,

I know that throughout the years I probably treated you unfairly and held you accountable for things that may not have been your fault. It took me a long time to come to terms with the breakup of my parents' marriage. At times, I blamed you. I thought it was your fault that my family would never again be together.

Now I know that my parents would've gotten divorced whether you were there or not. The biggest realization I've come to is that you all love me: Dad and you, Mom and Pat. I see now how lucky I am to have four parents who love me! We've had our ups and downs and will probably have more. But I respect you and understand more now than I did when I was five, when all of this had first happened.

Love,
Kelly (age nineteen)

---

Dear Stepfather,

I really don't know you well yet, even though you and Mom have been married for two years. You seem so harsh and cruel at times, and then you flip, and become loving and kind. I don't understand you.

You say you're a Christian, yet you forget that God said to love and respect your wife. You treat my mom so badly, it just kills me!

I hate how you're partial to my little brother, and yet you severely punish him. When your "perfect" grandson does the exact same things, you call him cute!

I helped raise my little brother, and now you won't let me have this kind of relationship with him anymore. You make me feel left out of the family. You reject me. My mom was *mine* first! But you forget this and act like she's your private property! I can tell that you despise me, but what have I ever done, other than be there first?

Why are you so hateful and mean? Why?

Corin (age nineteen)

Dear Pam,

I've been brought up to respect my elders and not to be rude. But I really need to get something off my chest. I don't respect you at all! How can I when you've made my dad's life miserable? You turned my loving father into an angry man that couldn't smile.

I know how you wouldn't leave my dad alone when you worked together. I know my dad is also responsible, but he is my dad. I will always love him, even if he did cave in to your constant sexual advances.

You tore my family apart. All you cared about was yourself and getting a husband for yourself and a dad for your kids, totally oblivious that this man already had a family! When my parents split, I was devastated and, of course, I blamed you.

The whole time you dated my dad, he was an angry and frustrated man. He sometimes took it out on us. Did you even know that your fighting with him was so out of control that it affected all of us?

I'm so glad that your three-year, off-and-on relationship with him and your brief marriage to him are finally over.

Without you in his life, my dad smiles again, which, in turn, makes me smile, too. It's too late for my parents, but I'm satisfied to have my dad returned to the loving man he always was. He's now dating a woman that lets him continue to love his children while loving her.

I'm so happy without you,
Chad (age nineteen)

Dear Barb,

In the beginning, our relationship was nonexistent. As time has gone by though, we've grown closer. I see that you and Dad really care about each other. I'm happy for you two. Seeing you love him gives me such a warm feeling!

Living on my own has helped me understand you more, because I'm without the influence of my mother, who is naturally bitter toward you. I myself am strong-minded and resisted you, but now I know that you're in my life for a reason.

Thank you for making me feel welcome anytime in your home. I enjoy Saturday bowling with you and Dad and my brothers because it helps me see you both in action. We can see that you're great for Dad.

Well, thanks for showing us that you're all right.

Love,
Russ (age twenty-two)

Dear Margaret,

I know that my stepdad loves me 'cuz . . . 'cuz . . . he kisses my mom!

James (age six)

Conclusion

# Some Final Words

Feelings ebb and flow—between children and their parents and stepparents, between parents and stepparents for one another. *But it is the commitment, the kindness, and the concern with which you treat one another that ultimately makes a relationship—and a family—last. In the end, it's the condition of one's heart that makes or breaks a marriage.*

Are you actively participating with God in character development? In Galatians 5:22, the apostle Paul says that the fruit of the Spirit (the result of God living in you) is "love, joy, peace, patience, kindness, goodness, faithfulness, gentleness and self-control."

***In the end, it's the condition of one's heart that makes or breaks a marriage.***

Are you daily attempting, through the power of God, to show the fruit of His Spirit in your life? Are you more concerned with being the person God wants you to be than with making your mate do the things you think he or she should do?

Here are some final powerful truths from God's Word. Meditate upon them whenever you feel helpless:

*Keep your servant also from willful sins;*
*may they [the sins] not rule over me.*
*Then will I be blameless,*
*innocent of great transgression.*
*May the words of my mouth and the meditation of my heart*
*be pleasing in your sight,*
*O Lord, my Rock and my Redeemer.*

*—Psalm 19:13–14*

*See if there is any offensive way in me,*
*and lead me in the way everlasting.*

*—Psalm 139:24*

*Teach me to do your will,*
*for you are my God;*
*may your good Spirit*
*lead me on level ground.*

*—Psalm 143:10*

*Being confident of this, that he who began a good work in you will carry it on to completion until the day of Christ Jesus.*

*—Philippians 1:6*

When things seem tougher than you can bear, or when the stepkids and/or the second marriage present challenges that seem impossible to live with, focus on these things:

*Who shall separate us from the love of Christ? Shall trouble or hardship or persecution or famine or nakedness or danger or sword? . . . No, in all these things we are more than conquerors through him who loved us. For I am convinced that neither death nor life, neither angels nor demons, neither the present nor the future, nor any powers, neither height nor depth, nor anything else in all creation, will be able to separate us from the love of God that is in Christ Jesus our Lord.*

*—Romans 8:35–39*

*Therefore we do not lose heart. Though outwardly we are wasting away, yet inwardly we are being renewed day by day. For our light and momentary troubles are achieving for us an eternal glory that far outweighs them all. So we fix our eyes not on what is seen, but on what is unseen. For what is seen is temporary, but what is unseen is eternal.*

*—2 Corinthians 4:16–18*

And lastly, the verse that could be the "theme verse" of stepparenting:

*Let us not become weary in doing good, for at the proper time we will reap a harvest if we do not give up.*

*—Galatians 6:9*

# Endnotes

## *Chapter 1: Blended Names*

1. Margaret Broersma, *Daily Reflections for Stepparents* (Grand Rapids: Kregel, 2003), 201–202.

## *Chapter 3: Blending Discipline*

1. Margaret Smith-Broersma, *Devotions for the Blended Family* (Grand Rapids: Kregel, 1994); Margaret Broersma, *Daily Reflections for Stepparents* (Grand Rapids: Kregel, 2003).
2. Margaret Smith-Broersma, *Devotions for the Blended Family.*
3. Marion Schooland, *Leading Little Ones to God* (Grand Rapids: Eerdmans, 1981).
4. Walter Wangerin, "Sacrificing My Son's Love," *The Lutheran,* January 2000, 6.

## *Chapter 4: Nurturing Your Marriage Relationship*

1. Dick Dunn, *New Faces in the Frame: A Guide to Marriage and Parenting in the Blended Family* (Nashville: LifeWay Press, 1997).

## *Chapter 6: Help in Blending—Good Counsel*

1. Ron Deal, *The Smart Stepfamily: Seven Steps to a Healthy Stepfamily* (Minneapolis, Minn.: Bethany House, 2002), 60.

### *Chapter 7: Blending Holidays and Traditions*

1. Gloria Gaither and Shirley Dobson, *Let's Make a Memory* (Dallas: Word, 1994).

### *Chapter 10: Loyalty Issues*

1. Dick Dunn, *New Faces in the Frame: A Guide to Marriage and Parenting in the Blended Family* (Nashville: LifeWay Press, 1997).
2. Ibid., 87.
3. Ibid.
4. Jane Nelsen, Cheryl Erwin, and H. Stephen Glenn, *Positive Discipline for Your Stepfamily* (Roosevelt, Calif.: Prima Publishing, 2000), 120.

### *Chapter 12: Blending Religions, Issues of Faith*

1. Leslie Parrott, *Saving Your Second Marriage Before It Starts* (Grand Rapids: Zondervan, 2001); Dick Dunn, *Willing to Try Again* (Valley Forge, Pa.: Judson Press, 1993).

### *Chapter 13: Etiquette for Blended Families*

1. Judith Martin, *Miss Manners' Guide to Excruciatingly Correct Behavior* (New York: Warner Brothers, 1982), 345.

### *Chapter 14: Blending Finances and Legal Matters*

1. Bob Burnes, *What Makes a Man Feel Loved* (Eugene, Ore.: Harvest House, 1998); Dennis and Barbara Rainey, *Building Your Mate's Self-Esteem* (Nashville: Thomas Nelson, Inc., 1995).
2. Ericka Lutz, *The Complete Idiot's Guide to Stepparenting* (Indianapolis: Alpha Books, 1998), 262.
3. Ibid.
4. *Stepping Stones for Stepfamilies,* vol. 5 (Kansas State University Agricultural Experiment Station and Cooperative Extension Service, August 1997), 3.
5. Ibid.
6. Ibid.
7. Ibid.

# Resources

## Books


Broersma, Margaret. *Daily Reflections for Stepparents.* Grand Rapids: Kregel, 2003.

Deal, Ron. *The Smart Stepfamily: Seven Steps to a Healthy Stepfamily.* Minneapolis, Minn.: Bethany House, 2002.

Dunn, Dick. *Willing to Try Again.* Valley Forge, Pa.: Judson Press, 1993.

———. *New Faces in the Frame: A Guide to Marriage and Parenting in the Blended Family.* Nashville: LifeWay Press, 2003.

Parrott, Leslie. *Saving Your Second Marriage Before It Starts.* Grand Rapids: Zondervan, 2001. These are practical workbooks for "him" and "her."

Ricci, Isolina. *Mom's House, Dad's House: Making Two Homes for Your Child.* New York: Simon and Schuster, 2003.

Smith-Broersma, Margaret. *Devotions for the Blended Family.* Grand Rapids: Kregel, 1994.

Wallerstein, Judith, and Sandy Blakeslee. *What About the Kids? Raising Children Before, During, and After Divorce.* New York: Hyperion, 2003. This is an excellent source for understanding what children go through in a divorce and remarriage. Dr. Wallerstein is the definitive expert on the subject of children and divorce. She has done extensive, long-term studies on this subject.

Wallerstein, Judith, Julia Lewis, and Sandy Blakeslee. *The Unexpected Legacy of Divorce.* New York: Hyperion, 2000.

See the Stepfamily Association web site (URL below) for many other practical books and materials.

## Stepfamily Web Sites

Here are good places to both learn about the issues and get advice:

1. Stepfamily Association of America
   http://www.stepfam.org
2. Stepdads.com
   http://www.stepdads.com
3. The Other Mother
   http://www.othermother.com
4. Second Wives Club
   http://www.secondwivesclub.com
5. The Law Offices of Jeffery M. Leving, Ltd.
   http//www.dadsrights.com